Supporting Disorders of Learning and Co-ordination

This revised and updated third edition, previously titled *The Effective Teacher's Guide to Dyslexia and Other Learning Difficulties (Learning Disabilities)*, unravels the complexity of specific learning difficulties in an accessible and user-friendly way.

Each chapter provides key information about the disorder in question, giving a clear definition before discussing prevalence, causal factors, identification, and assessment and provision. Implications for the curriculum and related assessment, pedagogy, resources, therapy/care, and school and classroom organisation are explained, allowing providers to reflect and adapt their practice in response to the needs of the individual. The book informs effective provision, with the aim of encouraging the best achievement and personal and social development for children and young people.

The book authoritatively and lucidly addresses issues associated with

- impairment in reading/dyslexia,
- impairment in written expression/dysgraphia,
- impairment in mathematics/dyscalculia, and
- developmental co-ordination disorder/dyspraxia.

Recognising the importance and the challenge of multi-professional working, the book relates provision to the roles of parents and carers alongside that of the practitioner. Underpinned by research and widely held professional judgement, this will prove a practical, readable, and inspiring resource for professionals in the UK, US, and elsewhere including teachers, therapists, psychologists, and students entering these professions.

Michael Farrell is a widely published private special education consultant. He works with children, families, schools, local authorities, voluntary organisations, universities, and government ministries. He has published books extensively with Routledge, with recent titles including *The Special Education Handbook* (4th edition) and *Debating Special Education*.

The Effective Teacher's Guides Series, all by Michael Farrell

The Effective Teacher's Guide to Behavioural and Emotional Disorders: Disruptive Behaviour Disorders, Anxiety Disorders and Depressive Disorders, and Attention Deficit Hyperactivity Disorder, 2nd edition
PB: 978-0-415-56568-4 (Published 2010)

The Effective Teacher's Guide to Sensory and Physical Impairments: Sensory, Orthopaedic, Motor and Health Impairments, and Yraumatic Brain Injury, 2nd edition
PB: 978-0-415-56565-3 (Published 2010)

The Effective Teacher's Guide to Autism and Communication Difficulties, 2nd edition
PB: 978-0-415-69383-7 (Published 2012)

The Effective Teacher's Guide to Moderate, Severe, and Profound Learning Difficulties (Cognitive Impairments), 2nd edition
PB: 978-0-415-69387-5 (Published 2012)

Supporting Disorders of Learning and Co-ordination: Effective Provision for Dyslexia, Dysgraphia, Dyscalculia, and Dyspraxia, 3rd edition
PB: 978-1-032-01271-1 (Published 2022)

Supporting Disorders of Learning and Co-ordination

Effective Provision for Dyslexia, Dysgraphia, Dyscalculia, and Dyspraxia

Third edition

Michael Farrell

Routledge
Taylor & Francis Group

LONDON AND NEW YORK

Third edition published 2022
by Routledge
2 Park Square, Milton Park, Abingdon, Oxon OX14 4RN

and by Routledge
605 Third Avenue, New York, NY 10158

Routledge is an imprint of the Taylor & Francis Group, an informa business

First edition published by Routledge 2006
Second edition published by Routledge 2011

British Library Cataloguing-in-Publication Data
A catalogue record for this book is available from the British Library

Library of Congress Cataloging-in-Publication Data
Names: Farrell, Michael, 1948- author.
Title: Supporting disorders of learning and co-ordination : effective provision for dyslexia, dysgraphia, dyscalculia and dyspraxia / Michael Farrell.
Other titles: Effective teacher's guide to dyslexia and other learning difficulties (learning disabilities)
Description: 3rd edition. | Abingdon, Oxon ; New York, NY : Routledge, 2022. | Series: The effective teacher's guides | Revised edition of: The effective teacher's guide to dyslexia and other learning difficulties (learning disabilities). 2nd ed. 2012 | Includes bibliographical references and index.
Identifiers: LCCN 2021019870 (print) | LCCN 2021019871 (ebook) | ISBN 9781032012735 (hardback) | ISBN 9781032012711 (paperback) | ISBN 9781003177975 (ebook)
Subjects: LCSH: Dyslexia--Great Britain. | Dyslexic children--Education--Great Britain. | Learning disabled children--Education--Great Britain.
Classification: LCC LC4710.G7 F37 2022 (print) | LCC LC4710.G7 (ebook) | DDC 371.91/440941--dc23
LC record available at https://lccn.loc.gov/2021019870
LC ebook record available at https://lccn.loc.gov/2021019871

ISBN: 978-1-032-01273-5 (hbk)
ISBN: 978-1-032-01271-1 (pbk)
ISBN: 978-1-003-17797-5 (ebk)

DOI: 10.4324/9781003177975

Typeset in Bembo
by Taylor & Francis Books

Contents

About the author

Michael Farrell was educated in the United Kingdom. After training as a teacher at Bishop Grosseteste College, Lincoln, and obtaining an honours degree from Nottingham University, he gained a Master of Arts degree in education and psychology from the Institute of Education, London University. Subsequently, he carried out research for a Master of Philosophy degree at the Institute of Psychiatry, Maudsley Hospital, London, and for a Doctor of Philosophy degree under the auspices of the Medical Research Council Cognitive Development Unit and London University.

Professionally, Michael Farrell worked as a head teacher and as a lecturer at London University. He managed a national psychometric project for City University, London, and directed a national initial teacher-training project for the United Kingdom Government Department of Education. For over a decade, he led inspections of mainstream schools and of special schools and units (boarding, day, hospital, psychiatric). Currently, he works with a range of clients as a private special education consultant. The countries where he has lectured or provided consultancy services include China, Japan, the Seychelles, Australia, Peru, Sweden, and the United Kingdom.

Among his books, which have been translated into European and Asian languages, are *Looking into Special Education* (Routledge, 2014) and *Investigating the Language of Special Education* (Palgrave Macmillan, 2014).

Preface to the third edition

It is a great pleasure to be writing the preface to *Supporting Disorders of Learning and Co-ordination* (third edition). When I heard from readers and led conferences using the previous edition of this book, then called *The Effective Teacher's Guide to Dyslexia and Other Learning Difficulties*, it became increasingly clear that it spoke to a wide range of people.

Certainly, these included teachers, head teachers, classroom assistants, and school governors and managers. But equally important were psychotherapists, audiologists, speech and language therapists/pathologists, and many others. Parents of children and young people with a disorder of learning or co-ordination were important participants.

In this new edition, I am pleased to better reflect this wide range of interest not only in the book's title but in its content. The book has also been updated to reflect further developments in research and understanding.

Michael Farrell
Herefordshire, United Kingdom
drmjfarrell@bulldog1870.plus.com

Chapter 1

Introducing disorders of learning and co-ordination, and provision

Introduction

Here, I introduce disorders of learning and co-ordination. The chapter explains aspects of these disorders such as 'prevalence' and 'causal factors', and, regarding provision, discusses examples such as, 'pedagogy', 'therapy', and 'organisation'. I outline the content and structure of the book, highlighting features of this new edition, and explain for whom the book is intended.

Disorders of learning and co-ordination

Disorders of learning and co-ordination discussed in the present book are

- impairment in reading/dyslexia,
- impairment in written expression/dysgraphia,
- developmental co-ordination disorder/dyspraxia, and
- impairment in mathematics/dyscalculia.

These disorders are sometimes called 'specific' in that, being circumscribed, they do not imply a generalised difficulty in learning (as does for example cognitive impairment). The designation goes back some years. In the US, 'specific learning disability' is one of the designated disability codes (code 9) reflecting categories of disability under federal law which include impairment in reading, impairment in written expression, and impairment in mathematics (20 United States Code 1402, 1997). In England, a similar classification, 'specific learning difficulties', comprises dyslexia, dyscalculia, and dyspraxia (Department of Education and Skills, 2005).

DOI: 10.4324/9781003177975-1

Aspects of disorders of learning and co-ordination

In each of the subsequent chapters on different types of disorders, I discuss definitions, prevalence, causal factors, and identification and assessment.

Definitions of disorders

Defining a disorder as clearly as possible is naturally important. Definitions may involve criteria such as those set out in the *Diagnostic and Statistical Manual of Mental Disorders Fifth Edition* also known as *DSM-5* (American Psychiatric Association, 2013). These in turn relate to identifying and assessing the disorder. However, these definitions are debated. For some commentators, the term 'dyslexia' can be misleading when interpretations separate it from difficulties with reading that many professionals and researchers consider central (Elliott and Grigorenko, 2014).

Prevalence

In the present context, prevalence refers to the 'amount' of a disorder in a population at a specified time. Often, it is given as a percentage (or proportion) of the population in question. 'Point prevalence' therefore concerns the percentage at a specific point in time, such as a stated date. 'Period prevalence' refers to the percentage over a longer time between two specified dates. As to the population, it might be the wide general one, or a smaller subgroup such as people in a certain age band. A related term, 'incidence' is a measure of the new cases of a disorder arising in a population in a specified period, for example a day, a month, or a year. Such information enables health care and education providers to plan provision.

Estimates of prevalence of a condition such as impairment in reading can vary widely. People may disagree about the nature of the condition, and therefore about the criteria used in identifying and assessing it. Where there is such disagreement, it affects confidence in what represents suitable provision.

Causal factors

Because it may not be possible to identify what directly causes a disorder, the expression 'causal factors' is used. This allows attention to be drawn to several potentially relevant influences. With impairment in reading, researchers have examined many contributary candidates, including phonological processing/deficit, visual processing, rapid naming, and auditory processing.

Identification and assessment

Identification and assessment of types of disorders is linked to definitions and related criteria. Where a disorder has been defined and criteria have been developed for it, it is unsurprising that this is used in identification and assessment. Related to this is the use of psychometric tests, observations of the individual, and discussions with others.

Co-occurrence of disorders

Some disorders commonly co-occur. To take just one example, the co-occurrence of developmental co-ordination disorder with attention deficit hyperactivity disorder is about 50% (American Psychiatric Association, 2013). Where disorders arise together, it may be because of common underlying causal factors. Or the disorders may relate to shared difficulties with 'underlying' skills such as attention and memory.

Aspects of provision for disorders

In later chapters, as well as aspects of disorders, provision for them is also discussed regarding curriculum and related assessment, pedagogy, resources, therapy/care, and organisation.

Curriculum refers to the content of what is to be presented to or made available for an individual. It is devised with the intention that a student will gain knowledge, build a skill or skills, and develop certain attitudes and values. It is the 'what' of enabling learning and development. Such a framework also involves structure, like the content being set out in a certain order (for example from easy to harder aspects).

Where it is important to know that something has been learned, curriculum-related assessment comes in. If an individual has been learning aspects of phonics, then assessments may be carried out to see if these have indeed been acquired.

Pedagogy concerns methods of teaching that enable learning. It may involve encouraging the use of senses to enhance learning – looking, listening, touching, and so on. The learner may be encouraged to practice a skill in small steps and build from these into more complex skill patterns. Guidance (through discussion) may be given to help an individual develop attitudes like respect for others.

Resources refer to the materials, equipment and other aids used to enhance learning and development. Examples are pencil grips, computers and software, rulers, microscopes, gymnasium equipment such as wall bars and vaults, and maps.

Therapy refers to provision involving specialists in certain areas of development. They include speech and language therapists/pathologists, physiotherapists, psychotherapists, psychologists (clinical, school/ educational), physicians, and nurses.

Care relates to therapy. It concerns ensuring that the health and well-being of an individual are enhanced and involves teachers, teaching/ classroom assistants, medical and nursing professionals, and others.

Organisation has to do with grouping arrangements made to encourage learning and development. It may refer to learners interacting in pairs or small groups. On a wider scale, it can denote the organisation of a setting where a larger number of learners are present. This might be a school, clinic, tuition centre, or similar, where decisions are made about grouping learners, for example, according to age.

Provision and effectiveness

Aspects of provision such as 'curriculum' and 'organisation' interrelate. Provision may comprise programmes or approaches in which content, pedagogy, and resources overlap. However, distinguishing these aspects can help providers to systematically review what they offer.

Provision is expected to be 'effective' in enhancing learning and development. This implies that there is evidence from studies, or professional consensus among those using the approaches, of their benefits. Important to establish are the efficacy and anticipated outcomes of a particular practice, whether expected outcomes match an individual's needs, and potential risks of protracted intensive interventions, including threats to family cohesion. Approaches can be evaluated drawing on evidence-based practice. They are also informed by professional judgement, and the views of the individual with the disorder and of their family or carers. Provision for a particular individual should encourage progress, development, and well-being.

Accommodations and modifications to programmes

A distinction is made between special education accommodations and modifications. Essentially, accommodations are physical or environmental changes an educator makes to the learning setting. Examples are giving more time to complete a task, allowing short breaks within the allocated time, changing the layout of the room or part of it, and using computer software to 'read' text to the student. These enable the learner to work round a potential difficulty.

Modifications may be made where learners have profound cognitive or other difficulties. They change the core programme by using a parallel curriculum that does not include all standards typical of the age grade in question. It may involve changes in standards required, courses followed, and timing of programmes. This may include lower-level reading, eliminating specific standards, and modifying the curriculum.

Order and structure of subsequent chapters

Remaining chapters of this book each cover a disorder of learning or co-ordination:

- impairment in reading/dyslexia;
- impairment in written expression/dysgraphia;
- impairment in mathematics/dyscalculia; and
- developmental co-ordination disorder/dyspraxia.

New to this edition is a chapter on multi-professional working reinforcing the importance of professionals understanding each other's role and pulling together with a common purpose.

Each chapter typically includes a definition of the disorder, prevalence, causal factors, and identification and assessment. This is followed by a description of provision, such as projects, approaches, and schemes found to be effective and supported by professional judgement, brought together under a framework of curriculum and related assessment, pedagogy, resources, therapy/care, and organisation. Each chapter offers thinking points to encourage discussion and reflection. Key texts are mentioned for further reading. References are included at the ends of chapters so that they are available if an individual chapter is copied or purchased electronically.

Proposed readers

Proposed readers include those involved in education, namely teachers, head teachers, classroom assistants, and school governors and managers. Also central are psychologists, audiologists, speech and language therapists/pathologists, and many other professionals, as well as parents and carers.

Conclusion

Impairment in reading/dyslexia, impairment in written expression/dysgraphia, developmental co-ordination disorder/dyspraxia, and impairment in mathematics/dyscalculia may be grouped as disorders of learning and co-ordination. They can be understood in relation to their definitions, prevalence, causal factors, identification and assessment, and co-existing conditions. Provision can be identified in terms of curriculum and related assessment, pedagogy, resources, therapy and care, and organisation.

References

American Psychiatric Association (2013) *Diagnostic and Statistical Manual of Mental Disorders Fifth Edition (DSM-5)*. Washington DC, APA.

Department of Education and Skills (2005) *Data collection by special educational need*(2nd edition). London, DfES. https://dera.ioe.ac.uk/7736/.

Elliott, J. G. and Grigorenko, E. L. (2014) *The Dyslexia Debate*. New York, Cambridge University Press.

Legal citations

20 United States Code 1402, 1997 (Title 20 – education chapter 33 education of individuals with disabilities, subchapter 1, 'general provisions' section 1402 Office of Special Education Programs) https://law.justia.com/codes/us/1997/title20/chap33/ subchapi/sec1402.

Chapter 2

Impairment in reading/dyslexia

Introduction

Reading involves word reading skills, reading fluency, and understanding/ comprehension. Impairment in reading/dyslexia is difficult to define, a situation exacerbated by researchers using different criteria to characterise it. Owing to this, estimates of prevalence vary widely.

Impairment in reading involves cognitive causal factors. These are phonological processing/deficit, auditory and visual processing, rapid naming, short term and working memory, and attention. There are also possible neurobiological causal factors, but they are less well understood. Identifying and assessing reading impairment includes using commercial assessments.

Provision addresses three aspects: phonics learning, reading fluency, and reading comprehension. Provision for phonics learning involves explicit phonics teaching, generalising phonological skills to reading, and group approaches that support phonics awareness and understanding. Interventions to improve reading fluency include RAVE-O (Retrieval, Automaticity, Vocabulary elaboration, Engagement with language, Orthography), and structured reading programmes that are flexibly linked with reading fluency approaches. Improving reading comprehension involves, general strategies, vocabulary instruction, and multi-component approaches to strategy instruction.

Such provision relates to the curriculum and assessment, pedagogy, resources, therapy, and organisation.

Reading and reading processes

Receiving e-mails and text messages, poring over a newspaper magazine or book, agreeing a contract, navigating a supermarket, and understanding labels are part of everyday life. In all these examples, and many

DOI: 10.4324/9781003177975-2

more, modern society demands that its members can read. It is under-standable therefore that difficulties with reading and what can be done to help people who experience them attract continuing interest and research.

Given that fluent, accurate reading draws on processes and skills, it fol-lows that problems with reading involves such processes. Reading has been described as, 'a process of constructing meaning from print' involving 'decoding' and 'comprehension' (Pullen and Cash, 2011, p. 409).

Decoding requires the reader to master subskills including

- phonological awareness and an understanding that written letters represent sounds which are blended into words (the alphabetic principle),
- recognising words,
- understanding concepts involved in print,
- developing vocabulary, and
- spelling (Ibid., paraphrased).

Reading *comprehension* involves

- recognising words,
- reading fluently, and
- accessing and using background knowledge relevant to understanding passages of text (Ibid., paraphrased).

Key aspects of reading therefore include word reading skills, reading fluency, and understanding/comprehension. As we shall see later, developing these are central features of provision.

Definition of impairment in reading

The widely used *Diagnostic and Statistical Manual of Mental Disorders Fifth Edition (DSM-5)* (American Psychiatric Association, 2013, pp. 66–74) proposes a category of 'specific learning disorder'. This may involve com-binations of impairment in reading, written expression, or mathematics.

Specific learning disorder broadly concerns 'Difficulties learning and using academic skills'. Importantly, attempts have been made to tackle these difficulties with targeted interventions, but they have persisted. The disorder begins during school age years and the 'symptoms' are not better accounted for by other conditions or factors such as intellectual disabilities or 'inadequate educational instruction'. (Note that *DSM-5* makes it clear that difficulties arising from poorly targeted and inadequate 'instruction' must not be mistaken for a specific learning disorder.)

Regarding reading, for at least six months there must have been 'symptoms' of 'inaccurate or slow and effortful word reading' and 'difficulty understanding the meaning of what is read'. Reading is 'substantially' below levels expected for the individual's age causing 'significant interference' with academic performance, work performance, or daily living. This is indicated by the results of individually administered standardised achievement measures and 'comprehensive clinical assessment'. The subskills involved are word reading accuracy, reading rate or fluency, and reading comprehension (Ibid., pp. 66–67).

The vague notion of reading achievement being 'substantially below' expectations requires further clarification. One way of achieving this is through using the standard deviation of reading scores. This is a statistical indication of variation showing the spread of scores about the mean in a 'normal distribution'. A reading score of two or more standard deviations below the expected level would be considered 'substantially below'. Sometimes, for example where the disorder has significantly affected performance in the test of general intelligence, a reading score falling one standard deviation below the expected level may be sufficient.

A strength of the use of the term 'specific learning disorder' is that it conveys a complex disorder which may involve combinations of impairment in reading, written expression, or mathematics. A difficulty in using the expression 'dyslexia' is that it may be seen by some commentators as a separate condition detached from other seemingly related disorders. Accordingly, *DSM-5* (American Psychiatric Association, 2013, p. 67) refers to dyslexia as 'a pattern of learning difficulties characterised by problems with accurate or fluent word recognition, poor decoding, and poor spelling abilities' (Ibid.). Related criteria specify that any additional difficulties, such as in mathematics reasoning should be specified (Ibid.).

Prevalence

Prevalence estimates of reading problems vary widely. For 'specific learning disorder', which, as we have seen, can include combinations of disorders of reading, written expression, and mathematics, they range from 5% to 15% for school aged children (American Psychiatric Association, 2013, p. 70). Estimates of dyslexia range from 5–8% to 20% (Mather and Wending, 2012; Shaywitz, 2005). Regarding reading comprehension, research found that about 3–4% of readers with 'adequate' word reading skills (above 90 standard score) had poor comprehension (below 90 standard score) (Klingner, Vaughn, and Boardman, 2015, p. 4).

Why do prevalence estimates vary so much? Impairment in reading and related terms are defined and put into practice in different ways. Also, the strictness of the criteria used varies. Where impairments are brought together as 'specific learning disorders' researchers may not distinguish within this group impairments in reading, written expression, and mathematics.

Cognitive causal factors

Reading problems have underlying them various interacting difficulties with cognitive (mental) processes (Snowling and Hulme, 2011, p. 4). Prominent among these are

- phonological processing/deficit,
- auditory processing,
- visual processing,
- rapid naming,
- short term memory and working memory, and
- attention.

Phonological processing/deficit

Phonological processing is important to reading, and someone with impairment in reading may often experience problems with such processing, that is, a phonological deficit.

Phonological knowledge enables us to understand that changing a speech sound in a word alters meaning. This allows us to distinguish between such words as 'cat' and 'hat' or 'bit' and 'big'. Hearing our own speech, we modify it as necessary to make the required word. Our phonological system helps make the process become automatic. It lays down a phonological representation of the speech sound sequence. We draw on this cognitive representation when developing awareness of the different sounds in a word.

In reading English, the speech sounds (there are 44 of them) are linked to written marks (graphemes). This enables us, usually as children, to develop a link between sound and written marks, a so-called phoneme–grapheme correspondence.

In line with this understanding of phonological processing, Tunmer (2011) proposes several aspects:

- phonetic perception (encoding phonological information);
- phonological awareness (accessing phonological information and performing mental operations on it);

- lexical retrieval (retrieving phonological information from semantic memory which involves the meaning of words);
- short term verbal recall (retaining phonological information in working memory); and
- phonological recoding (translating letters and their patterns into phonological forms) (Ibid., p. x, paraphrased).

Having set out the complex nature of phonological processing, we can now consider the impact of problems with it. A core deficit in phonological processing may be a common cause of reading difficulties (Elliott and Grigorenko, 2014). Children with dyslexia may have problems processing spoken words in a precise manner because cognitively they are not fully laying down representations of speech sounds.

As the representations become degraded, it becomes harder to acquire phonological skills such as phonological awareness and decoding links between letter and sound. Weak phonological decoding may mean that the learner struggles to link the spoken and visual counterparts of printed words. This in turn weakens the storage of high-quality representations of word spellings which can impair rapid word identification and reading fluency (Ibid., pp. 42–49).

Researchers reviewed studies looking at relationships between phonemic awareness, short term verbal memory, children's word reading skills, and rime awareness, (Melby-Lervåg, Lyster and Hulme, 2012). (Linguistically, a rime is that part of a syllable that comprises its vowel and any consonant sounds following it. In the word 'tub' the rime is 'ub'.) The researchers found that poor readers, compared with typically developing younger readers at the same reading level, had a large deficit in phonemic awareness (Ibid.).

Also, various interventions based on a hypothesised phonological deficit have been developed. These have been found to improve the skills and performance of struggling readers at least in the short term (Olson, 2011).

However, the phonological deficit hypothesis is not a complete explanation. Not all children with reading impairments experience a phonological deficit. Indeed, children with poor phonological skills can go on to develop good reading skills (Catts and Adlof, 2011). Nevertheless, phonological deficit is likely one of several interacting deficits leading to reading impairment (Ibid.).

Auditory processing

Auditory processing refers to a sequence in which a sound is taken in through the ear and conveyed to the brain's language area for interpretation. A disorder or delay in auditory processing does not imply abnormal hearing. It is a matter of processing rather than hearing.

Auditory processing likely influences phonological awareness. Impaired auditory processing tends to limit our ability to reflect on the sounds and words we hear, perhaps partly causing phonological deficits.

Various auditory processing deficits appear to be more likely in children and adults with reading impairment (Elliott and Grigorenko, 2014, p. 68). Training programmes can improve the auditory task performance of children with auditory processing deficits, but there is less evidence that this improves reading (McArthur, 2009).

Visual processing

Visual processing concerns the brain's ability to use and interpret visual information from our surroundings. Translating light energy into a meaningful image involves many brain structures and higher-level mental processes. When reading, visual analysis involves identifying each letter, encoding its position in the relevant word, and (when reading a sequence of words), establishing an 'attentional window' focusing attention on a single word.

A feature partly explaining visual difficulties affecting reading is 'abnormal crowding' which impairs the visual discrimination of nearby letter contours. Features unrelated to the 'target' may be incorrectly integrated so that letter discrimination is made harder (Schneps et al., 2013).

A study assessed the binocular vision of 26 'dyslexic children' using visual tests and ophthalmological tests (concerning the anatomy and functioning of the eyes). Where assessments required visual convergence, and ability to look with both eyes was unstable, the children had less control of their eye movements (Castro, Salgado, Andrade, Ciasca, and Carvalho, 2008).

A 'magnocellular' (large cell) visual pathway may relate to reading problems. This pathway appears to detect movement, contrast, and rapid changes in the visual field. Lowered sensitivity in this system may limit the suppression of visual information so that images last too long on the retina. Therefore, visual information accumulates, reducing visual acuity (clarity of vision) especially the precise recognition of small details. Reduced visual acuity leads to impaired reading.

In line with a magnocellular theory, people with dyslexia may experience lowered sensitivity to rapidly presented stimuli, which can lead to poor performance in visual tasks and problems reading (Stein, 2008; Wright and Conlon, 2009). However, it is considered that there is insufficient evidence of a possible magnocellular deficit to base treatment on it (American Academy of Pediatrics, 2009).

Rapid naming

Some children with reading difficulties have problems with 'rapid automatized naming', the ability to quickly name items (visual stimuli) they already know. In research demonstrating this, people are shown a series of familiar items such as letters, numbers, colours, or objects, and asked to name them. The naming speed tends to correlate with difficulties in reading (Norton and Wolf, 2012).

There is debate about how much poor naming speed and phonological deficit might sometimes combine creating a 'double deficit'. More practically, it is doubted whether naming speed can be increased, and even if it could, whether this would produce better reading performance (Ibid.).

Short term memory and working memory

Short term memory passively stores information. Working memory concerns storage and processing, and involves a central executive system and controlled processes relating to attention. Both types of memory have been linked to reading problems. Opinions differ about whether memory processes can be improved directly and, even if they can, whether this would improve reading.

Educators sceptical about improving memory processes by direct intervention may concentrate more on teaching relevant skills of reading and spelling. In any event, teachers are likely to take account of any difficulties a learner has with memory. They might avoid overloading the learner with excessive information that could be presented in parts. Educators may also teach students memory strategies like grouping information in clusters (Gathercole and Alloway, 2008).

Attention

In the present context, 'attention' refers to focusing one's awareness on something while shutting out other stimuli. If someone is slow transferring attention from one item to another, it may create difficulties in dealing with sequences of visual or auditory information (Lalier, Donnadieu, Berger, and Valdois, 2010). Accordingly, some individuals with impairment in reading may find it hard to disengage from visual and auditory stimuli presented in quick sequence.

Regarding auditory processing, slowness in shifting attention might interfere with the perception of rapid streams of speech. This could hinder the development of phonological representations and impair reading. Turning to visual processing, a visual attention span deficit might limit the number of letter string elements that the reader can process simultaneously again impairing reading (Bosse, Tainturier, and Valdois, 2007).

Genetic and neurobiological causal factors in reading

There is 'limited knowledge and understanding of the role genetic factors play in reading development' (Elliott and Grigorenko, 2014, p. 121). Research indicates that impairment in reading has a genetic component. However, genetic knowledge cannot presently enable such impairment to be separately identified or point to individualised types of intervention.

Neurobiology concerns the biology of the nervous system. Regarding brain anatomy and physiology, imaging enables the shape and size of brain features and brain functioning to be studied. This indicates differences between individuals with impairments in reading and typically developing readers. However, such research does not differentiate a dyslexic sample from a larger group of poor decoders. Neither can brain based measures determine a sample of poor readers who are likely to benefit from a particular type of intervention (Elliott and Grigorenko, 2014, pp. 88–122).

Identification and assessment

Where there are concerns about a learner's reading, educators, school/educational psychologists, and speech and language pathologists/therapists may review a range of evidence. Identifying and assessing difficulties with reading may include

- developing a profile of the learner's mistakes such as their omitting words or confusing one letter with another,
- bringing together from different sources an account of how the learner reads, for example, whether they hesitate over words, and
- establishing whether the learner prefers reading silently or aloud and whether one preference leads to better reading comprehension than the other.

Reading skills

Commercial assessments of 'dyslexia' and subskills of reading are available, standardised for the country concerned. Sampling skills that relate to reading and to impairments in reading, they include assessments of phonological skills and rapid naming of visual stimuli.

Dynamic Indicators of Basic Early Literacy Skills (DIBELS 8) (University of Oregon, 2020) takes a curriculum-based approach to assessing reading comprising a series of standardised assessments for learners in Kindergarten through sixth grade. *DIBELS 8* has six sub tests aimed at assessing component skills of reading. These are letter naming fluency (LNF), phonemic segmentation fluency (PSF), nonsense word fluency (NWF), word reading fluency (WRF), oral reading fluency (ORF), and a maze.

Reading and word assessments may be part of a wider set of assessments. The *Woodcock Johnson IV Test of Achievement* is a comprehensive set of tests exploring strengths and weaknesses in cognitive, oral language and academic abilities. It includes a standardised measure of sight word knowledge (Woodcock, Schrank, McGrew, and Mather, 2014).

Reading comprehension

Reading comprehension is not assessed solely with one procedure. Rather, several approaches are generally used, tailored to specific circumstances. Assessments include tests standardised on a wider population, informal reading inventories, interviews with the learner, questionnaires, and observations. Learners can be asked to retell what has been read or can be encouraged to talk about what they are thinking as they read (Klingner, Vaughn, and Boardman, 2015, p. 42). Taken together, several such assessments show strengths and weakness in reading comprehension. Using a range of carefully chosen assessments can reveal different insights into the learner's problems.

The *Gray Oral Reading Test (GORT-5)* (Widerholt and Bryant, 2012) covers a wide age range from 6 to 23 years 11 months. Administered individually by a specialist teacher, it takes about 20 to 30 minutes to complete. The test uses 16 reading passages which are placed in a developmental sequence. Each passage is followed by five multiple-choice comprehension questions.

The *Woodcock Reading Mastery Test* (Woodcock, 2011) is used for ages ranging from 4 years 6 months to 79 years 11 months. It takes between 15 and 45 minutes to administer individually. The test assesses reading readiness and reading achievement. Its subtests concern phonological awareness, listening comprehension, letter identification, word identification, rapid automatic naming, oral reading frequency, word attack, word comprehension, and the comprehension of passages.

Provision

Approaches to reading impairment tend not to try to improve in isolation deficits and skills underpinning difficulties (Friedmann, Kerbel, and Shvimer, 2010). Rather, they tackle reading skills and knowledge directly, not ignoring underlying skills, but expecting such skills to improve in the context of more practical, direct learning of reading. Accordingly, interventions tend to focus on provision for

- phonics learning,
- reading fluency, and
- reading comprehension.

Phonics learning

Approaches to enhance phonics learning include

- explicit phonics teaching,
- approaches to generalise phonological skill to reading, and
- group approaches supporting phonics awareness and understanding.

Explicit, systematic phonics teaching

Explicit and implicit phonics

Explicit, systematic phonics teaching begins with phonics and builds up to words. On the other hand, *implicit* phonics teaching begins with words and their context and works back to the phonics, as necessary.

Explicit, systematic phonics teaching has been found to be effective in helping people young and old with impairments in reading to learn to decode words effectively (Roberts, Torgsen, Boardman, and Scammacca, 2008). See also https://www.readinghorizons.com/reading-stra tegies/teaching/phonics-instruction/what-is-systematic-and-explicit-p honics-instruction.

The Phono-graphix® Reading Intervention and Instruction Programme

In the phonemic code of written English, each sound in a spoken word is represented by some part of the written version. The Phono-graphix® Reading Intervention and Instruction Programme (The Phono-graphix® Reading Company, 2020) centralises these phonetic code implications. It teaches the phonological skills of blending, segmenting, and manipulating phonemes, which are required to use a phonemic code. Phono-graphix® systematically, explicitly teaches correspondences in sound-to-symbol relationships.

Generalising phonological skills to reading

An approach intended to generalise learners' skills to reading is the PHAST Track Reading Programme. PHAST stands for **PH**onological **A**nd **S**trategy **T**raining. Aiming to encourage skills in reading, comprehension, spelling, and writing, it builds on two components.

The first, Phonological Analysis and Blending/Direct Instruction trains the learner in sound blending and left to right phonological decoding strategies. The second component, the Word Identification Strategy Program, helps develop metacognitive word identification strategies (for example, identifying words by analogy, or looking for familiar parts of the word).

A sequence of strategies is used in conjunction with initial phonological training. One is rhyming, introducing up to 120 key words which enable other words to be read (as 'and' enables reading 'hand', 'sand', and so on). A further strategy, 'game plan', enables the learner to apply all the other strategies.

Developed for children with impairment in reading, the PHAST Track Reading Programme allows for individual or group teaching. Designed as a 70-hour lesson plan, classes last one hour, four to five days a week for 14 to 18 consecutive weeks. An adaptation, PHAST PACES, was developed for high school readers and young adults. See http://dyslexia-ca.org/pdf/files/lovettmar07/lovett2.pdf for an overview.

Group approaches supporting phonics awareness and understanding

What is the most suitable setting for systematic, explicit phonics teaching and ensuring students generalise phonics skills to wider reading? Initially it may require individual or small group teaching. However, supporting activities and approaches can take place in larger groups.

Elements of such support are basic pedagogic principles. They include drawing direct attention to features of language to raise awareness and recognition, fostering an interest in language and how it works, and encouraging learners to practice certain sounds, words, and expressions that they may find difficult. Encouraging careful listening is also important. Along with speech, aids like pictures or objects can be used to help memory by presenting information in several sensory modes – auditory, visual, and tactile.

Educators and speech-language pathologists can ensure that learners/clients improve their awareness of sounds and sound sequences conveying meaning in speech. Students can practise using and recognising key sounds that change meaning. Examples are 'er' at the end of words such as 'fast', 'soft', and 'hard' that convey an increased quality; or 'un' at the beginning of words such as 'tidy' or 'dressed' that create an opposite.

Similarly, speech comprehension practice can be used to help learners notice key sounds that convey meaning and signal changes in meaning. Educators can teach learners to listen for and recognise the sound 's' at the end of a word when it signals a plural as in 'cat' and 'cats'. Educators can help a learner's speech comprehension by using visual aids like a picture of one 'cat' and several 'cats' when saying the respective words. Similarly, objects such as toys or everyday items can also be used to supplement speech and clarify the purpose of the activity.

Where new vocabulary is introduced, students can be encouraged to take an interest in a word or phrase. Teachers and speech pathologists can explicitly teach and check the learners' understanding of various aspects of vocabulary: word meaning, its grammatical function, and its phonological make-up. Phonological aspects may include asking questions: 'How do the sounds of the word break up?'; 'How do the sounds of the word blend back together?'; and 'What are the syllables of the word?'.

In a school, improving awareness and understanding of phonics can be planned across the curriculum. This helps to ensure all teachers, not just literacy specialists, recognise the importance of support for reading and understanding. It can enhance subject teaching and improve reading because all members of staff contribute.

Reading fluency

Among approaches to improve reading fluency are

- general strategies for reading fluency,
- structured reading programmes that are flexibly linked with reading fluency programmes, and
- Retrieval, Automaticity, Vocabulary elaboration, Engagement with language, Orthography (RAVE-O).

General strategies for reading fluency

General approaches for improving reading fluency use broad pedagogic principles. These include repetition and practice, developing familiarity with the material to be read, building confidence through nurturing success, using a rich variety of attractive materials that generate readers' interest, and creating an encouraging environment.

Before reading a passage, a few selected key words from the text can be examined in preparation. They can be read, used in a sentence, spoken aloud, briefly discussed and in such ways made familiar. Working in pairs using flash cards can add interest to this activity. With this preparation, reading the passage soon afterwards becomes easier. Reading material should be chosen so that it does not require too many preliminary key words. Otherwise, it is harder for the reader to remember the words, and the point is lost.

Where learners feel anxious about reading, teacher and student can begin by talking about a picture accompanying the text. This can lead to discussing what the passage is likely to be about and provide some of the key words that will emerge. If this is done regularly, anxiety of thinking that a reading session is always about diving straight into challenging text is reduced and progress can be improved. More broadly, it is important that the environment is relaxed but purposeful. Mistakes should be seen not as failures but as the opportunity to try again and get it right.

Learners can read the same material several times. If this is not overdone to the point of boredom, it can make reading a particular passage easier so that the learner gains confidence. The reader begins to recognise the rhythm and pace that is missed if reading is anxiously stilted.

Material that is interesting and stimulating to readers increases motivation. Finding out what sort of material engages the reader can give pointers. Short passages can be used initially. A limerick or other short verse, pages from a well-illustrated book, comics with speech bubbles and captions, extracts from a familiar story, passages of information on computers, are just a few examples.

Learners should be encouraged to read at a manageable pace at which they can understand, which may be slow at first. At the same time, they should be guided to keep the pace steady. As reading fluency improves, pace will increase.

As an educator, you can check that when using computer text, a reader is adopting a font style and size and text spacing that aids reading fluency. This is particularly important where a reader has difficulties with visual processing but can also help other readers chose a font and spacing with which they feel more confident, so long of course as it helps their reading including fluency. Please also see articles at Read and Spell on fluency strategies at https://www.readandspell.com/fluency-strategies-for-struggling-readers.

Structured reading programmes linked with reading fluency programmes

If learning to read accurately and being able to read fluently are both important, combined interventions make sense. Accordingly, structured reading programmes have been used with approaches for improving reading fluency.

One intervention provided groups of two or three second-grade students (age 7 to 8 years) with a daily 45-minute sessions for six months. It developed instruction using the *Responsive Reading Instruction Programme* (Denton and Hocker, 2006) and other suitable fluency interventions as appropriate. These were used flexibly within a framework of lesson components according to learners' individual needs. Researchers compared a group that experienced the intervention with a group receiving typical school instruction. In word identification, phonemic decoding, word reading fluency, and comprehending sentences and paragraphs, the intervention group made significantly better progress. However, the two groups were similar in reading pseudo words, text reading fluency, and comprehending extended passages (Denton et al., 2013).

Such research suggests that combining approaches can lead to benefits, but that not all aspects of reading are equally enhanced. This underlines the importance of having flexible links between strategies so the overall approach can be adjusted to improve aspects of reading where progress was weaker.

Retrieval, Automaticity, Vocabulary elaboration, Engagement with language, Orthography (RAVE-O)

RAVE-O is a programme to develop reading fluency by helping learners to achieve automaticity in word knowledge. It is designed for certain readers in second grade (age 7 to 8 years) through fifth grade (age 10 to 11 years). They will be reading below grade-level and/or will struggle with fluency or 'naming speed'. RAVE-O may also benefit English-language learners. To achieve fluency, learners must be able to automatically retrieve letter patterns and their related sounds. Importantly, they must be able to automatically access the meanings of words, roots and affixes, and the role of words in sentences.

In small groups, learners read text to form new knowledge and ideas, and to improve reading achievement. RAVE-O connects phonics, spelling, vocabulary, grammar, and morphology, to aid reading fluency and comprehension. Sessions build skills in the sounds that form the structure of words, in recognising common letter patterns, and in developing knowledge of vocabulary. Learners practice parts of speech and discuss the roots and suffixes of words. Eventually these skills are connected to reading passages of text. Wolf, Barzillai, Gottwald, Miller, and colleagues (2009) and https://www.voyagersopris.com/literacy/rave-o/overview provide an overview of RAVE-O and related evidence.

Reading comprehension

In examining reading comprehension, we look at general issues, vocabulary instruction, and multi-component approaches.

General points on reading comprehension

Success in reading comprehension assumes that learners have a good foundation of skills, knowledge, and understanding in phonics learning and reading fluency. Therefore, if there are problems with reading comprehension, it is important to make sure that the precursors have been securely laid down.

Even where a learner has a grounding in phonics and reading fluency, reading material must be pitched at the right level to enable comprehension. If reading material is too hard, a reader has to give attention to phonics and fluency so that comprehension is likely to suffer. The teacher can temporarily lower the reading challenge of the text being used to allow comprehension to develop. Familiar reading material can be used enabling attention to be focused on comprehension. A variation of finding easier or familiar reading material is that it can be read as a preparation for building up to more challenging text. This allows the reader to become familiar with the content before tackling the harder text.

Reading aloud and reading in pairs or small groups can aid comprehension. If someone else is reading, a particular student can follow the text, focusing on comprehension. When the student themselves is reading aloud, they are also hearing themselves read, adding an auditory dimension to aid comprehension. On the other hand, an individual might be anxious about reading aloud in front of others and understanding may be diminished.

Discussing what is being read aids comprehension of both stories and factual articles. Prior to reading students can be encouraged to think about the title of a piece and ask what the passage might be about and what aspects could be especially interesting. When reading, the learner can sometimes pause to discuss the content, and what might follow. Once material is finished, the reader can be asked to talk about it, paraphrase it, and express their opinion of it.

Vocabulary instruction

Vocabulary instruction where it improves understanding of word meaning contributes to reading comprehension. Vocabulary can be taught a few words at a time so that new concepts are introduced manageably and related to familiar concepts (Joseph, 2008, p. 1172).

Word meaning can be taught directly by introducing the word, providing a definition, giving examples of its use, and encouraging learners to use the word in context. Learners can make a visual 'map' or web to show links between the meaning of a target word, and related words. This can stimulate the learner to make related mental links. Sometimes a word's meaning can be remembered by linking it to a vivid or comical image that suggests what it conveys.

Multi-component approaches

We have already touched on general strategies aiding comprehension before, during, and after reading. Multi-component approaches develop this in a more structured way, helping learners use comprehension strategies while they are learning content from text. Three examples are: reciprocal teaching, transactional strategy instruction, and collaborative strategic reading. Each uses discussion with peers to help readers to comprehend, and to use independent reading strategies.

Reciprocal teaching involves prediction, summarising material, generating questions, and clarifying. These guide group discussions of material that has been read. As an educator, you initially model how to use the comprehension strategies. You then use prompts, questions, and reminders to support learners in using the strategies themselves while they are reading and discussing the text. Gradually as students become more competent, support is reduced. Prediction, summarising material, generating questions, and clarifying are used collaboratively and in dialogue to make the text meaningful and help learners absorb the strategies (Please see Klingner, Vaughn, and Boardman, 2015, pp. 173–179, for a summary).

In transactional strategies instruction, educators explain and emphasise approaches used by learners with good strategies. Gradually educators give learners responsibility for strategic processing, encouraging collaboration, and nurturing interpretative discussions. Teachers describe the processes both internal and external that they use while reading (predicting, visualising, inferring, summarising, monitoring for understanding, and activating existing knowledge). To encourage learners to transfer strategies, teachers indicate when and where they could be used, giving prompts and cues so that eventually students apply the strategies on their own initiative (Brown, 2008).

Collaborative strategic reading teaches learners to use comprehension strategies while working collaboratively in small peer groups on expository text. Teachers first present the strategies to the learner group using modelling, role playing, and speaking their own thoughts while reading or doing a related activity. As students begin to absorb the strategies, the teacher organises them into mixed cooperative learning groups. Each group member carries out a specified role while implementing the strategies with the others, for example as leader, or helping the group work out the meanings of difficult words (Klingner, Vaughn, and Boardman, 2015, pp. 184–192, provide a summary).

Curriculum and assessment, pedagogy, resources, therapy, and organisation

Having looked at a range of interventions, approaches, strategies, and programmes, it is now possible to draw together issues in relation to broad areas of learning and development. These are curriculum and assessment, pedagogy, resources, therapy, and organisation.

Curriculum and assessment

Where learners have impairment in reading and are taught in a school, the curriculum may emphasise language and reading by providing more time for these with necessary support. Within other curriculum areas such as science or history, the reading element will be an important focus of support.

Small steps of assessment may be used with language and reading to ensure that a student's progress is recognised. Within the wider curriculum there may be programmes encouraging phonics skills and understanding, reading fluency, and reading comprehension like those described earlier. These often combine curriculum content, approaches to pedagogy, and specific resources.

Pedagogy

Individual specialist tutoring may be necessary to accelerate the progress of learners with reading impairment. In teaching structured information such as phonics, pedagogy should be systematic and explicit. Multi-sensory teaching can help a learner remember new material. Educators model strategies and approaches, ensuring that students gradually adopt them so that support can be gradually lowered. Paired and small group discussion is used for example with reading comprehension. Encouragement and a supportive ethos are created to reduce any anxiety felt by learners.

Resources

Some assessments involve commercially developed tests. For some phonics-based interventions, commercially produced programmes are available.

Computer software that supports reading may also be used. Materials like printed lessons and computer activities associated with programmes may be employed. Photographs and objects are used to stimulate interest and aid memory for example in aspects of phonics teaching.

Therapy

A speech-language pathologist may work directly with individual learners or small groups. They may take a consultancy role supporting teachers and parents for example to help with learners' phonological difficulties.

Organisation

Supporting learners with impairment in reading is likely to involve small group work. Some will require intensive one-to-one sessions with a specialist tutor or speech-language pathologist. Such individual work may take place in a resource room, or tutoring room. Where individual work is necessary in a school, it should not prevent the learner experiencing a rich, relevant curriculum. Schools and clinics may offer training workshops for parents wishing to learn about their approaches and who may wish to continue them at home.

Conclusion

Reading involves word reading skills, reading fluency, and understanding/comprehension. Widely used guidance identifies impairment in reading as a 'specific learning disorder' which may involve combinations of impairment in reading, written expression, or mathematics. Where the term 'dyslexia' is used, guidance suggests that additional difficulties like reading comprehension or mathematics reasoning should be specified. Estimates of the prevalence of impairment in reading and dyslexia vary widely. Cognitive causal factors include phonological processing/deficit, auditory and visual processing, rapid naming, short term and working memory, and attention. There is limited understanding of the role of genetic factors in reading development. Identifying and assessing reading impairment includes the use of commercial tests.

Provision for reading impairment involves phonics learning, reading fluency, and reading comprehension. Phonics learning concerns explicit phonics teaching, generalising phonological skills to reading, and general group approaches supporting phonics awareness and understanding. Provision to aid reading fluency includes general strategies, structured reading approaches linked with reading fluency programmes, and

RAVE-O (Retrieval, Automaticity, Vocabulary elaboration, Engagement with language, Orthography). Among reading comprehension interventions are general strategies, vocabulary instruction, and multi-component approaches. All these aspects of provision relate to the curriculum and assessment, pedagogy, resources, therapy, and organisation.

Thinking points

What justifications are there respectively for using direct approaches to improving reading, and for tackling apparent underpinning skills deficits?

In a larger group setting, how can effective strategies to improve reading fluency and comprehension be encouraged?

Key texts

Brooks, G (2016) (5th edition) *What Works for Children and Young People with Literacy Difficulties?*

This book describes a wide range of interventions accompanied by evaluations of their effectiveness.

References

American Academy of Pediatrics (2009) 'Learning disabilities, dyslexia and vision'. *Pediatrics* 124, 837–844.

American Psychiatric Association (2013) *Diagnostic and Statistical Manual of Mental Disorders Fifth Edition (DSM-5)*. Washington DC, APA.

Bosse, M. L., Tainturier, M. J., and Valdois, S. (2007) 'Developmental dyslexia: The visual attention span deficit hypothesis'. *Cognition* 104, 198–230.

Brooks, G. (2016) *What Works for Children and Young People with Literacy Difficulties? The Effectiveness of Intervention Schemes*. 5th edition. Dyslexia-SpLD Trust. http://www.interventionsforliteracy.org.uk/wp-content/uploads/2017/11/What-Works-5th-edition-Rev-Oct-2016.pdf.

Brown, R. (2008) 'The road not yet taken: A transactional strategies approach to reading comprehension'. *The Reading Teacher* 61, 7, pp. 538–547 (April 2008). http://www.jstor.org/stable/20204627.

Castro, S. M., Salgado, C. A., Andrade, F. P., Ciasca, S. M., and Carvalho, K. M. (2008) 'Visual control in children with developmental dyslexia'. *Arquivos Brasilieros de Ofthalmologia* 71, 6, 837–840 (November–December).

Catts, H. W. and Adlof, S. (2011) 'Phonological and other language deficits associated with dyslexia' in Brady, S. A., Baze, D., and Fowler, C. A. (Eds.) *Explaining Individual Differences in Reading: Theory and Evidence* (pp. 137–151). New York, Psychology Press.

Denton, C. A. and Hocker, J. L. (2006) *Responsive Reading Instruction: Flexible Intervention for Struggling Readers in the Early Grades*. Longmont CO, Sopris West.

Denton, C. A., Tollar, T. D., Fletcher, J. M., Barth, A. E., Vaughn, S., and Francis, D. J. (2013) 'Effects of tier 3 intervention for students with persistent reading difficulties and characteristics of inadequate responders'. *Journal of Educational Psychology* 105, 3, 633–648.

Dyslexia Foundation of New Zealand (2008) *Dealing with Dyslexia: The Way Forward for New Zealand Educators*. Christchurch, New Zealand, Dyslexia Foundation of New Zealand.

Elliott, J. G. and Grigorenko, E. L. (2014) *The Dyslexia Debate*. New York, Cambridge University Press.

Friedmann, N., Kerbel, N., and Shvimer, L. (2010) 'Developmental attentional dyslexia'. *Cortex* 46, 1216–1237.

Gathercole, S. E. and Alloway, T. P. (2008) *Working Memory and Learning: A Practical Guide*. London, Sage.

Joseph, L. M. (2008) 'Best practices on interventions for students with reading problems' in Thomas, A. and Grimes, J. (Eds.) *Best Practices in School Psychology V: Volume 4* (pp. 1163–1180). Bethesda, MD, National Association of School Psychologists.

Klingner, J., Vaughn, S., and Boardman A. (2015) *Teaching Reading Comprehension to Students with Learning Difficulties*. 2nd edition. New York, Guilford Press.

Lalier, M., Donnadieu, S., Berger, C., and Valdois, S. (2010) 'A case study of developmental phonological dyslexia: Is the attentional deficit in the perception of rapid stimuli sequences amodal?' *Cortex* 46, 231–241.

McArthur, G. M. (2009) 'Auditory processing disorders: Can they be treated?' *Current Opinion in Neurology* 22, 137–143.

Mather, N. and Wending, B. J. (2012) *Essentials of dyslexia assessment and intervention* Hoboken, NJ, Wiley.

Melby-Lervåg, M., Lyster, S., and Hulme, C. (2012) 'Phonological skills and their role in learning to read: A meta-analytic review'. *Psychological Bulletin* 138, 322–352.

National Early Literacy Panel (2008) *Developing Early Literacy: Report of the National Early Literacy Panel*. Washington, DC, National Institute for Early Literacy.

Norton, E. S. and Wolf, M. (2012) 'Rapid automatized reading (RAN) and reading fluency: Implications for understanding and treatment of reading disabilities'. *Annual Review of Psychology* 63, 427–452.

Olson, R. K. (2011) 'Genetic and environmental influences on phonological abilities and reading achievement' in Brady, S. A., Baze, D., and Fowler, C. A. (Eds.) *Explaining Individual Differences in Reading: Theory and Evidence* (pp. 197–216). New York, Psychology Press.

The Phono-graphix® Reading Company (2020) *The Phono-graphix® Reading Intervention and Instruction Programme*. https://phono-graphix.com/.

Pullen, P. C. and Cash, D. B. (2011) 'Reading' in Kauffman, J. M. and Hallahan, D. P. (Eds.) (2011) *Handbook of Special Education*. New York and London, Routledge.

Roberts, G., Torgsen, J. K., Boardman, A., and Scammacca, N. (2008) 'Evidence-based strategies for reading instruction of older students with learning disabilities'. *Learning Disabilities Research and Practice* 23, 63–69.

Schneps, M. H., Thompson, J. M., Sonnert, G., Pomplun, M., Chen, C., and Heffner-Wong, A. (2013) 'Shorter lines facilitate reading in those who struggle PLoS One 8, 8, e, 71161 https://dash.harvard.edu/bitstream/handle/1/11855772/3734020.pdf?sequence=1.

Shaywitz, S. E. (2005) *Overcoming dyslexia*. New York, Alfred Knopf.

Shrank, F. A., Mather, N. and Woodcock, R. W. (2004) *Woodcock Johnson III Diagnostic Reading Battery*. Chicago, The Riverside Publishing Company.

Snowling, M. J. and Hulme, C. (2011) 'Evidence based interventions for reading and language difficulties: Creating a virtuous circle'. *British Journal of Educational Psychology*, 81–123.

Stein, J. (2008) 'The neurological basis of dyslexia' in Reid, H., Fawcett, A., Manet, F. and Siegel, L. (Eds.) *The Sage Handbook of Dyslexia* (pp. 53–76). London, Sage.

Tunmer, W. (2011) 'Foreword' in Brady, S. A., Braze, D., and Fowler, C. A. (Eds.) *Explaining Individual Differences in Reading: Theory and Evidence* (pp. ix–xiii). New York, Psychology Press.

University of Oregon (2020) *Dynamic Indicators of Basic Early Literacy Skills (DIBELS®): Administration and Scoring Guide*. 8th edition. Eugene, OR, University of Oregon. https://dibels.uoregon.edu/docs/materials/d8/ dibels_8_admin_and_scoring_guide_05_2020.pdf.

Widerholt, J. L. and Bryant, R. R. (2012) *Gray Oral Reading Tests – Fifth Edition (GORT-5)*. Austin, TX, PRO-ED. https://www.pearsonclinical.co.uk/Education/ Assessments/LiteracyAssessments/GORT-5/Gray-Oral-Reading-Tests-Fifth-Edition.aspx.

Wolf, M., Barzillai, M., Gottwald, S., Miller, L.*et al.* (2009) 'The RAVE-O intervention: Connecting neuroscience to the classroom'. *Mind, Brain and Education* 3, 2, 84–93.

Woodcock, R. W. (2011) *The Woodcock Reading Mastery Test*. 3rd edition. Circle Pines, MN, American Guidance Service. https://www.pearsonclinical.co.uk/Education/ Assessments/LiteracyAssessments/wrmt-iii/woodcock-reading-mastery-tests-third-edition.aspx.

Woodcock, R. W., Schrank, F. A., McGrew, K. S., and Mather, N. (2014) *Woodcock-Johnson IV*. Chicago, Riverside Publishing Company. https://info.riversideinsights.com/wj-ivhttps://educationelephant.ie/product/woodcock-johnson-iv-tests-of-achievement-uk-ire/.

Wright, C. M. and Conlon, E. G. (2009) 'Auditory and visual processing in children with dyslexia'. *Developmental Neuropsychology* 34, 330–355.

Chapter 3

Impairment in written expression

Introduction

Just as reading is a crucial skill in contemporary society, so writing is important for success in study, work, and everyday life. Before examining disorder of written expression, I outline the components of writing. These include spelling, grammar and punctuation/capitalisation, and written composition. Disorder of written expression is then defined in terms of spelling accuracy, correctness of grammar and punctuation, and clarity/organisation.

I give estimates of the prevalence of the disorder. Causal factors are examined regarding problems with spelling, and difficulties with punctuation accuracy and capitalisation, written grammar, and written expression. Assessments are discussed in relation to spelling accuracy, grammar and punctuation, and writing composition.

Provision for spelling is described involving multi-sensory aspects, Directed Spelling Thinking Activity, and target words. For grammar, I discuss direct teaching, modelling, and the use of the learner's own writing. Punctuation and capitalisation approaches are examined. They are systematic, based on assessments, adjusted according to individual needs, and combine explicit teaching with opportunities for applying the necessary skills and knowledge. I describe provision for writing composition namely, developing self-regulation strategies, reducing task demands, using frameworks for writing, writing for a purpose, teaching reading and writing combined, and computer-aided learning.

Finally, implications for the curriculum and assessment, pedagogy, resources, therapy, and organisation are outlined.

Components of writing

Written language comprises several components:

DOI: 10.4324/9781003177975-3

- handwriting;
- vocabulary;
- spelling;
- usage; and
- written composition/text structure.

Handwriting involves fine motor skills, letter memory, and the ability to form letters. If a computer keyboard is used instead of writing by hand, fine touch skills are needed to use the keys, and memory of letters is required to recognise them, although the need to form letters by hand is made unnecessary. Handwriting is discussed in the context of developmental co-ordination disorder in Chapter 5.

Vocabulary involves word knowledge, word retrieval, and morphology. Morphology concerns the study of the form of words and phrases. More specifically, it involves understanding word formation in language like inflection (for example, a change in tense), derivation, and compounding.

Spelling is a complex accomplishment. It implicates as well as morphology already mentioned, semantics (the meaning of words), orthography (the system of writing), and phonology (the sounds of language).

'Usage' embraces punctuation, and capitalisation and grammar. In this context, grammar is usually subdivided into syntax and morphology. Syntax refers to how words and other linguistic elements are combined into constituents such as clauses or phrases. As already mentioned, morphology involves understanding word formation in language such as inflection, derivation, and compounding.

Written composition also called text structure comprises cohesion and coherence of writing, narrative, and expository text. (Mather, Wendling, and Roberts, 2009, pp. 8–30 and Figure 2.2).

Key aspects of writing, namely spelling, usage (grammar and punctuation/capitalisation), and written composition arise in impairment of written expression.

Definition of impairment in written expression

In the *Diagnostic and Statistical Manual of Mental Disorders Fifth Edition (DSM-5)* (American Psychiatric Association, 2013, pp. 66–74) is a description of the essential features of 'impairment in written expression'. This is presented within the context of specific learning disorder which may involve combinations of impairment in reading, written expression, or mathematics.

In its wider sense, specific learning disorder concerns 'difficulties learning and using academic skills'. Within the definition it is specified that despite targeted interventions having been used to tackle these difficulties they have persisted. Specific learning disorder begins during school-age years and its indications are not better accounted for by other conditions or factors such as intellectual disabilities or 'inadequate educational instruction'.

Subskills of disorder of written expression set out in the diagnostic criteria involve spelling, grammar and punctuation, and written composition. They are

- spelling accuracy,
- grammar and punctuation accuracy, and
- clarity or organisation of written expression (Ibid., p. 67).

In line with guidance in *DSM-5* (American Psychiatric Association, 2013), Berninger (2009) discusses learning disability relating to writing. He mentions the processes of memory for word meaning and working memory. Also mentioned are problems with spelling, grammatical structures, morphological awareness, organising information, and committing thoughts to writing (Ibid.).

Prevalence

When research is carried out to try to establish the prevalence of impairment in written expression, it does not often separate the impairment from impairment in reading or mathematics, making prevalence is difficult to determine.

A study in Brazil investigated the prevalence of *DSM-5*-specific learning difficulties (American Psychiatric Association, 2013, pp. 66–74) in samples of students. Educated in second to sixth grades, they came from median cities in four geographic regions. Prevalence rates of SLDs for writing were 5.4% (Fortes et al., 2016).

Causal factors and associated factors relating to impairment in written expression

Offering a direct cause of impairment in written expression is difficult and it is more accurate to speak of features which may contribute, that is, 'causal factors'. Also, while some factors are 'associated with' impairment in written expression, the nature of the relationship is unclear. Bearing this in mind, related to disorder of written expression are

- spelling accuracy,
- grammar and punctuation accuracy, and
- clarity or organisation of writing.

Spelling

Because correct spelling requires knowledge of phonology, orthography, morphology, and semantics, difficulties with these affect spelling. For example, for some learners, difficulties remembering orthographic patterns can impair spelling that involves irregular patterns (Mather, Wendling, and Roberts, 2009, p. 111).

Grammar and punctuation

For some students, difficulties with punctuation accuracy and capitalisation may reflect problems recognising and learning the necessary rules and applying them to their own writing (Mather, Wendling, and Roberts, 2009, p. 141).

Problems with written grammar may arise from lack of opportunity to see and read examples of accepted grammatical forms. Lacking opportunity or encouragement to try writing simple pieces, moving on to longer ones, the student may have struggled. With guidance, such activities enable grammar to be developed (Ibid., p. 143).

Writing composition

Given the complexity of written expression, many areas of the brain are likely to be implicated. Executive deficits and working memory deficits, which have been associated with poor sentence coherence and lexical cohesion may be particularly important. However, any educational implications of brain imaging findings are unclear (Pugh et al., 2006)

Learners struggling with writing may have associated problems. These may include difficulties with attention, self-regulation, and memory, including working memory, and language and reading skills. Struggling writers tend to be weaker in their knowledge of the genres, devices, and conventions of writing. Unsurprisingly perhaps, they also tend to be less motivated. Among more social and contextual influences associated with weak writing skills are family poverty and poor instruction. (Also see Graham and Harris, 2011, pp. 424–426.)

Identification and assessment

Identifying and assessing apply to the key areas of spelling accuracy, to both grammar and punctuation, and to writing composition.

Assessments of spelling accuracy

Spelling problems show themselves in several common ways. Confusion about words ending in 'er', 'or', and 'ar' may result in spellings such as 'docter' or 'doctar' for doctor. Sounds such as 's' and 'z' may cause problems. Spelling may be inappropriately phonetic ('cof' for 'cough'). The middle or end of a word may be missed out. Some words may be spelled in different ways at different times ('nesesery', 'nececary', and 'nesacary' for 'necessary'). Letters or syllables may be written in the wrong order. In response the assessor (psychologist, specialist teacher, regular teacher) may construct a profile of the sorts of errors the student makes relative to the above characteristics.

Informal assessments of spelling can be made using phonics charts of commonly used letters and blends. One example is a 'check off chart' (Mather, Wendling, and Roberts, 2009, p. 223, Figure 8.5). It covers

- consonants,
- initial digraphs (such as 'ch' in chip),
- initial consonant blends ('bl', as in 'black' and 'cl' as in 'club'),
- initial digraph blends ('sch' as in 'school'),
- final consonant blends ('lt' as in 'melt'),
- final digraphs and trigraphs ('ct' as in 'fact' and 'tch' as in 'match'), and
- final digraph blends ('nth' as in 'seventh').

Also used are commercially available standardised spelling assessments which may be a part of broader tests including reading and writing. An example is the *Wide Range Achievement Test (WRAT5)* (Robertson and Wilkinson, 2017). It covers the age range 5 to adult and takes about 15 to 25 minutes to administer for ages 5 to 7 and around 35 to 45 minutes for ages 8 and above. As well as subtests for word reading, sentence comprehension, and maths computation, the assessment has a spelling test which measures the ability to write letters and words from dictation without a time limit.

Assessments of grammar and punctuation

Cloze tests can help reveal accomplishment and difficulties with grammar. Consider that a student is told that a boy visited the shop yesterday. They are then asked to complete the cloze sentence 'Yesterday Tom ... to the shop'. Completing the task correctly shows understanding of past tense. These assessments might be accompanied by pictures or demonstrations to make clear what is being asked. In this way, cloze procedure assessments can establish a learner's understanding of speech parts and how they are used.

As a curriculum-based assessment, a teacher may use the criterion of 'correct writing sequences' covering spelling accuracy, grammar, punctuation, and capitalisation. This begins at the start of a writing sample and looks at each successive pair of writing units. A writing unit in this context is a word or an 'essential' punctuation mark. Credit is given for a writing unit that is spelled correctly, is grammatically correct, and makes sense within the context of the sentence. Capital letters must also be used appropriately. (Mather, Wendling, and Roberts, 2009, p. 234–238, provide a full description of the scoring system.)

Assessments of writing composition

Among assessments of writing are analytic scales and primary trait scales. Analytic scales provide scores on aspects of writing and can be interpreted to inform instruction. Aspects include ideas, organisation, sentence structure, and vocabulary. Primary trait scales provide scores based on the main purpose of the writing assignment being assessed. In a 'for and against' piece of writing the quality of the argument can be judged. In a story, plot development can be rated.

Writing and Reading Assessment Profile (WRAP) is an informal profile that includes assessment of writing. It enables educators to gather information on learners' literacy development and behaviours. This information is used to analyse and interpret reading and writing samples, select suitable literacy resources, and support skills and strategies enhancing literacy.

Provision for spelling

General issues – emphasising spelling clusters or using motivational context

When teaching and supporting spelling with children generally, approaches can either emphasise explicit direct instruction, or use the context in which the word arises. Direct instruction allows similarities in spellings to be highlighted to aid memory. For example, groups of words can be taught with similar spellings such as 'ill' as in bill, fill, hill, mill, pill, and so on. Once you recall the '-ill' part of the spelling you can produce several, sometimes many, words correctly. This gives a sense of achievement and boosts confidence, precious commodities for students who are having difficulties. On the negative side, drill can be boring and unmotivating.

A contextual approach rather teaches the spelling of a word when it is needed, and the student is motivated to remember it because they want to use it. On the downside, context does not give the opportunity to develop from a required word to clusters of words that have the same spelling sequence. Given that there are weaknesses and strengths with either approach, they are in practice often used together or at different times according to the perceived needs of the student.

All this applies to learners in general. However, individuals with impairment in written expression tend to learn better with intensive practice to help them remember the spelling securely. If the strategies are tilted too far towards learning from context, this practice is reduced, hindering spelling.

Drawing on phonics knowledge, a student can develop a grasp of phonologically recognisable spellings and make plausible attempts like 'hows' for 'house'. Eventually however the learner will have to move on from this to being able to check if a word looks correct (visual checking) based on knowledge of how other words are spelled. A learner with impairment in written expression will likely require much support at this phase.

Multi-sensory approaches

Various multi-sensory aids are used to teach spelling. This can involve speaking, hearing, seeing, and movement so that approaches involve speech-motor, kinaesthetic, visual, and auditory memory. Underpinning this is a broad pedagogic principle that memory and recall is improved if the learner can draw on several memory sources linked together. Associated with this the educator uses material and examples that interest and motivate the student and are familiar to them.

Teaching early letter sounds can be linked to what the learners knows, illustrating the sounds with pictures or objects. These are taught phonetically as the sound the letter makes rather than the pronunciation of the letter name. For example, 'a' pronounced as in 'cat' not as in 'cape'. If the learner is interested in or has pets, the sound 'c' can be linked with 'cat' and perhaps a picture of their own cat. Similarly, with 'd' and 'dog'. Other items that interest the learner can be used for this early work to build confidence and competence. Examples are letter sounds that can be illustrated by sports items, and objects and pictures linked to the student's hobbies. When links have been made with the letter sound and the item or picture, the learner will gradually visualise the aid on seeing the letter and will recall the letter sound accordingly.

Developing from learning letter sounds, the teacher can give learners cards to place in front of them and on which the letters are written. The teacher then talks about the letter sound and its shape, leading to basic word building. Using the first few letters that have been introduced, the teacher helps the student develop words like 'pat', 'mat', 'cat', and so on.

To help visual recall educators can show learners a written word and ask them to look carefully at it and remember as much as possible. Then the word is removed from view, and prompt questions are asked like, 'How many letters were there in the word?', 'What was the first letter?', 'What was the last letter?', or 'Were any of the letters the same?'.

Auditory recall of words can also be encouraged. Rhymes, poems, and songs enjoyably help to highlight the sounds of words. Younger learners can clap out syllables. Students can group words according to their sound, as with 'dog', 'bog', 'log'. A learner with auditory difficulties might not hear the similarities of words taught in clusters to aid spelling ('wish', 'dish') so the teacher must ensure that they notice the common rhyme, 'ish'.

The learner may finger draw letters in a sand tray to emphasise their shape and sequence. Progressing to tracing smaller letters, this leads to writing letters on paper. The learner can say and sound out phonetically regular words to embed this, using speech-motor memory as they articulate the word, and auditory memory as they hear the sounds.

Using 'look-say-finger trace-cover-write-check' can include looking at the word shape overall as well as individual letters. This recognises that the words may not be phonetically regular ones guessable from knowing their sounds. In 'simultaneous oral spelling', the learner says the letters while writing them, helping link kinaesthetic memory and auditory memory (See also Pollock, Waller, and Pollitt, 2004.)

Directed Spelling Thinking Activity

In the Directed Spelling Thinking Activity (e.g. AdLit.org, 2008) groups of learners are helped to contrast, compare, and categorise two or more words according to similarities and differences. Raising awareness of spelling patterns and more complex 'grapho-phonological' principles is the aim of this activity.

Consider that learners are examining words with a long /i/ sound as in 'thigh', 'by', and 'pie'. The educator encourages them to discover that the long /i/ can be made by the letters 'igh' as in not only 'thigh' but also in 'sigh'. It can be made with the letter, 'y' in 'by' but also in 'try' and 'cry'. The long /i/ can be made by 'ie' as in 'pie' and in words like, 'lie' and 'die'. Learners classify other similar words into groups or notice that they do not follow the common principle. To consolidate the learning, they might examine a passage in which are included examples of words conforming to the rule.

Target words for spelling

Target words are selected for particular attention to improve spelling. In line with recommendations for spelling programmes, target words can include high frequency core words, personal words, and word patterns illustrating some morphological or phonological principle. Personal words prepared with the learner will include ones that they use often in various contexts and may also be high frequency core words. In schools, older students and subject teachers can collaborate to make groups of words often used in subjects, like science, history, or geography.

When a learner has misspelled words in free writing sessions, only a few should be selected for correction. This avoids overloading the student with too many words to learn at one time, which is likely to be ineffectual and to sap vital confidence. It is also sensible to select more commonly used words for correction because they will have the greatest impact on future correct spelling. While some work on correcting spelling is necessary, repetition of spellings does not have to be tedious drill but can be made interesting. Short daily activities with weekly checks of progress will be more stimulating than long drills. Games, puzzles, and computer activities focusing on the important words can be motivating and helpful. Personalised lists can also be made. Mnemonics and word associations may help learners remember the spelling of target words. Encouragement, confidence building, and quick recognition of success are important themes of such work.

Resources or improving and consolidating spelling accuracy include computer software allowing the user to decide how words are grouped and to add chosen words. Other software employs a 'look, cover, write, and check' approach to learning spellings. The words are in 'families' or subject groups.

Among commercial spelling packages for the US market for example is *Spellography* (Sopris West, www.sopriswest.com). This teaches word roots and multisyllabic skills using various games and activities. *SpellWell* (Education Publishing Services, www.epsbooks.com), intended for learners in the second through to fifth grades, (ages 7/8 through 10/11 years) teaches skills cumulatively. Each book includes grade-suitable words that follow a particular spelling pattern or rule.

Provision for grammar and punctuation

Principles discussed below for grammar and for punctuation are good practice for all students. For those with disorder of written expression, learning may take longer and require more practice, application, and support.

Grammar

Learners struggling with grammar will tend not to learn its structures by a sort of absorption or pick up the necessary skills and knowledge from reading. Rather they tend to learn better with explicit instruction.

An educator can directly teach simple sentence patterns, and as the learner progresses these simple structures can be elaborated. Most rules are taught using the student's own writing. After modelling the acceptable forms of written grammar, the teacher can guide and praise the learner's attempts to do the same. An example might show how aspects of grammar can be conveyed using direct teaching/modelling, verbal practice, written practice, group and individual work, and encompassing the learner's own writing.

Consider that a teacher is dealing with sentence combining. The learner is shown how to combine two or more short sentences into a longer one, using direct teaching and modelling. The educator might then provide three or more sentences and ask a group of students to suggest how two or more might be combined, writing acceptable versions on a board. After such verbal practice, learners are asked to write several examples of combined sentences. Next working individually with learners, the teacher uses simple sentences from their work, to discuss how sentences might have been effectively combined perhaps by using conjunctions like 'and', 'but', and 'however'.

Another example is teaching the use of adjectives to enrich writing which begins with the teacher suggesting several nouns and giving examples of how each can be described by adjectives. Eliciting from the learners their own descriptive word, the teacher discusses how some of the suggestions are stronger or more appropriate than others. They then provide a sample of short sentences in which a weak adjective is used and ask for better examples. (Instead of a 'nice' cake, try a 'tasty' cake.) This can be done verbally at first and then supplemented by the teacher writing examples down. Several short sentences with weak adjectives can be provided which learners are asked to improve, or sentences may be used with blanks where an adjective might be inserted. Next working individually with learners and using simple sentences from their work, the teacher discusses how adjectives, or better adjectives could be used.

In checking and editing their work written on a computer, students can use grammar checking software. Grammatically-based cuing of words on such software can also help learners to expand their grammatical repertoire. Teachers can support learners having difficulties with grammar by discussing what is required and checking their understanding.

Commercially available resources for grammar include books and related material. An example is *Noun Hounds and Other Great Grammar Games* (Egan, 2001) which is intended for third through to sixth grade (ages 8/9 through 11/12 years).

Punctuation

Approaches for teaching punctuation and capitalisation are systematic, based on assessments, and are adjusted according to the requirements of each individual. Combining explicit teaching with opportunities for the student to apply the new learning, the strategies are carefully structured.

To improve a learner's punctuation, teachers need to teach punctuation rules and reinforce them within the context of their writing. This uses the principle of explicit instruction and applying what has been learned in a writing context. Learners must understand the rule and be able to apply it in their own writing activities. The most common punctuation marks are introduced first.

Accordingly, a justifiable sequence for instruction would be the following:

- full stop/period;
- question mark;
- comma;
- exclamation point/mark;
- apostrophe;
- quotation marks;
- colon;
- semi-colon;
- hyphen; and
- parenthesis.

It is possible to further break down the presentation and teaching of each punctuation mark. For example, teaching a full stop/period could involve a sequence of using a period after

- a sentence,
- a command,
- an abbreviation,
- numbers in a list,
- an initial, and
- letters or numbers in an outline (Mather, Wendling, and Roberts, 2009, p. 141–142).

Each punctuation mark may be systematically taught one at a time, drawing on explicit teaching, guided practice, and modelling. The teacher explains when and how the punctuation mark is used. Students gain practice using the punctuation mark in a sentence (or sometimes elsewhere as in a list). They are then encouraged to use the punctuation mark in their own writing. Where errors are made the teacher reviews the rules for using the mark and asks the learner to proofread their work for that particular mark (Ibid., p. 142).

Capitalisation can be taught in a similar way. Firstly, the learner's writing is assessed to establish what rules and examples they need to learn, and instruction is adapted accordingly. Using the principle of teaching the most common usages first, instruction might begin with

- first names and last names of people,
- the first words of a sentence,
- the word 'I',
- days and months of the year, and so on.

As with teaching spelling, words can be incorporated in which the learner has an interest to encourage better motivation.

Cloze procedures can be used. The student is given a passage in which some letters have been omitted. They must insert a small or a capital letter as required. The teacher can provide examples of the two 'missing' letters from which the learner choses (Ibid., pp. 142–143).

Resources used for developing correct punctuation include routinely available computer software. This offers alternative suggestions where it appears punctuation is incorrect or where it makes the expression unclear.

Provision for writing composition

The work and writing of learners having disorder of written expression tends to have certain features. Students may do little planning before they write and carry out minimal monitoring and evaluation of their work. Compositions tend to be short, with little detail or elaboration. Spending little time writing essays, learners may require prompting to do more. Difficulties with the mechanics of writing (spelling, punctuation, and shaping letters) further reduces the amount that is produced. Students' revisions of their own work focus on mechanical aspects and neatness rather than compositional aspects of writing. Interventions take account of this.

Developing self-regulation strategies

'Self-regulated strategy development' teaches learners with difficulties in writing to use the same types of strategies as more competent writers. As a 'cognitive strategies' instruction model, it aims to enhance students' strategic behaviour, self-regulation skills, content knowledge, and motivation. The following guidance draws on the approach described in research which involved students who were struggling writers, including students with disabilities (Harris, Graham, and Mason, 2006).

Outside the regular classroom, an assistant teaches small groups planning/writing strategies for persuasive writing and for story writing. For example, with persuasive writing, a general strategy is introduced involving

- picking a topic,
- organising ideas before writing, and
- writing and saying more while writing (continuing planning while writing).

Learners are taught a strategy for organising ideas:

- generating ideas;
- selecting from them; and
- organising them according to basic elements of persuasive writing.

Assessing an earlier piece of their writing, students evaluate aspects to give a baseline. Modelling how to use the strategies by 'thinking aloud', the assistant enables the learner to listen and understand. Before student begin the piece of persuasive writing, they are reminded to use all the basic elements. When the writing task is finished, they discuss what has helped. They develop several self-statements to use while they write. Assistant and learner write the next piece together setting objectives, using self-statements, and graphing their performance. Gradually the assistant withdraws support.

Reducing task demands

Reducing task demands helps to build learners' confidence by providing initial success. In story writing, the teacher can provide the beginnings of a series of sentences in a writing frame. This can be tailored to the learner's interests.

- When the light faded quickly, we found ourselves on the moor, without food or water and …

- At first, we …
- Then we took stock and realised …
- So, we made a …

To aid a learner's fluency in writing longer pieces of work and bypass the need to use a dictionary, the teacher can provide key words likely to arise, or that the learner asks for.

Reducing task demands can help a learner's note taking/dictation, a complex skill that is challenging for anyone. Where learners struggle to concentrate on what is being said at the same time as keeping hand-writing legible, they could reduce demands by writing down only key words. At the end of the dictation, the teacher gives the learner a copy of their notes to go through highlighting the key words identified. This forms a revision aid and a basis for reading the notes.

Reducing task demands enables the learner to concentrate on and improve upon smaller aspects of the overall task. The educator provides the structure for other aspects of the work, so the student completes a finished product. Gradually, supports are faded out so that the learner can carry out the whole process.

Frameworks for writing

Supporting frameworks for writing gets the learner started, gives direction to a task, and builds confidence. Educators encourage a learner's under-standing of the processes of developing ideas for writing, composing, and editing. Processes are modelled, posing questions that the learner can later use to structure their own attempts. Questions for generating ideas for a fictional story might be, 'Who is in the story?', 'Where does it happen?', 'What is the main event?', or 'What happens, first, next, finally?'.

In composing a non-fiction piece where the ideas have been generated, the teacher can model setting out the ideas in an understandable order. Questions might be, 'What are the main ideas?', 'Which should be first?', or 'What should come last?'. In composition each main idea can be taken in turn and expanded into a sentence or two.

In editing, the teacher shows the learner how to check if the structure and shape of the piece of writing is good, whether paragraphs are used effectively, if grammar is clear, and if punctuation and spelling are correct.

Writing for a purpose

Writing for a purpose aids motivation and gives an incentive to produce good quality work. It might involve writing a letter of thanks to a visitor, contributing to a newsletter, designing then writing a poster, writing to a distant friend, formulating a set of instructions for a piece of equipment, or sending e-mails. Other purposes include making shopping lists for projects or events, writing to the local newspaper, applying for a job, creating a story book for young children, composing letters on behalf of elderly and infirm people in a local residential home, or preparing a cooking recipe.

As well as being motivational, such work requires learners to consider requirements of writing for different audiences, a very subtle skill. At first, it may be easier to judge the audience if they are people that the learner has met.

Teaching reading and writing together

Self-regulated strategy development approaches for reading and writing were used in a study by Mason, Snyder, Sukhram, and Kedem (2006). Educators adopting this approach would act as follows. Students are taught a reading strategy (acronym TWA) involving the following:

- Think, before reading about the author's purpose, about what you want to know and what you want to learn.
- While reading, think about reading speed, linking knowledge, and rereading parts.
- After reading, think about the main ideas, summarising information, and what you learned.

Learners must be able to use the TWA strategy independently to produce a written outline and talk about the main points of what they have read. The educator then teaches the writing strategy helping students apply the information gleaned from their reading, under the (rather weak) mnemonic PLANS:

- Pick goals,
- List ways to meet goals,
- And make
- Notes, and
- Sequence them.

All this breaks the required task of planning what to write into more manageable subtasks making it easier for learners to use what they have read.

Resources for writing composition

Software packages are helpful at different stages of writing a piece of work: planning, composition, checking and correcting, and publishing. They help users develop and organise ideas, employing diagrams, allowing ideas to be arranged which helps to structure essays. Templates can be used for different areas of knowledge such as science and history. Some programmes provide partial or complete sentences to support writing, allowing personalised 'cloze procedure' exercises to be created.

Software enables users to hear, through synthetic speech, the sentences that they are constructing as they are being typed. This can reassure learners that what they are writing makes sense, and, where it does not, allows them to go back and check accuracy. Once writing is completed, text can be highlighted and a 'read aloud – speech' tool used to hear a synthetic voice read the whole text.

Commercially available material includes approaches using the framework in *Write Traits®* incorporating ideas, details, organisation, sentence fluency, voice, and conventions. Great Source (www.greatsource.com) provides such materials and workshops. *Language Circle/ Project Read Written Expression Curriculum* (www.projectread.com) offers a systematic multi-sensory approach to teaching writing skills.

Curriculum and assessment, pedagogy, resources, therapy, and organisation

Curriculum and assessment

In the setting of a school, tuition centre, or similar institution, writing is clearly central to other subjects and areas of learning likely to be taught, such as English, history, and science. Attainment in these subjects may be lower than is age typical where written responses are required. In the balance of subjects that are provided, writing may be emphasised to encourage and support students' progress in it. Planning across the whole curriculum will help to ensure that other subjects and areas of learning contribute to supporting literacy. For example, key words may be identified that will be explained and reinforced in other curriculum areas. Small steps of assessment may be used to recognise progress in written expression and related areas of learning.

Pedagogy

Interventions to improve spelling include multi-sensory approaches, Directed Spelling Thinking Activity, and focusing on target words.

Grammar is improved by using direct teaching/modelling, verbal practice, written practice, group and individual work, and encompassing the learner's own writing. Punctuation and capitalisation teaching is systematic, based on assessments, shaped to individual needs, and combines explicit teaching with opportunities for application. Pedagogy for writing composition involves developing self-regulated strategies, reducing task demands, using frameworks for writing, writing for a purpose, and teaching reading and writing in conjunction.

Resources

To aid spelling, computer software is available, sometimes mimicking strategies used generally. Commercial packages are used which may teach spelling skills through games and activities. Also available are commercially produced resources for grammar, for example, focusing on teaching a specific part of speech. Regarding punctuation, computer software routinely has punctuation correction facilities and can make suggestions for punctuation. In writing composition, computer software packages help users develop and organise ideas, employing diagrams and templates. Computer synthetic speech facilities allow a learner to hear what is being written both as it is written and at the end. Bought materials may use approaches that are systematic and may be multi-sensory.

Therapy

There appears to be no distinctive therapy necessary for the aspects of disorder of written expression discussed in the present chapter. For the movement aspects of written expression, there are therapeutic implications for physical therapy/physiotherapy, which are discussed in the Chapter 5.

Organisation

Individual, paired, and small group work all contribute to improving written expression. Group settings may be organised to encourage learners to share their writing with others. For example, writing may be edited and developed in pairs or groups.

Thinking points

You may wish to consider when and how to emphasise (for particular students) essential skills learning, which may lead to observable progress, or learning in context, which may be more meaningful.

Key texts

Gunning, T. G. (2013) *Assessing and Correcting Reading and Writing Difficulties.* 5th edition. Boston, MA, Allyn and Bacon.

Well-grounded in theory and research, this practical book for teachers has ideas and lesson plans for helping with literacy including strategies for developing word recognition skills, vocabulary, and comprehension.

Mather. N., Wendling, B. J., and Roberts, R. (2009) *Writing Assessment and Instruction for Students with Learning Disabilities.* 2nd edition. San Francisco, CA, Jossey-Bass/ John Wiley.

This well-structured book considers handwriting, spelling, usage, vocabulary, and text structure using extensive examples of students' writing. Some chapters give examples of learners' writing and guidance on its assessment.

Conclusion

Components of writing include spelling, grammar and punctuation/ capitalisation, and written composition. Disorder of written expression is defined in terms of spelling accuracy, grammar and punctuation accuracy, and clarity or organisation of written expression.

A Brazil study sample of students from the second to sixth grades (ages 7/8 through 11/12 years) in median cities from four geographic regions found prevalence of specific learning disorder for writing of 5.4% (Fortes et al., 2016).

Turning to causal factors, difficulties with knowledge of phonology, orthography, morphology, and semantics, hinder spelling. Poor punctuation accuracy and capitalisation may reflect problems recognising and learning the necessary rules and applying them to writing. Problems with written grammar may arise from lack of opportunity to develop literacy more generally. With written expression, possible causal factors range from executive deficits and working memory deficits to family poverty and poor instruction.

Identifying and assessing apply to the key areas of spelling accuracy, grammar and punctuation, and writing composition. Informal assessments, records of patterns of errors, phonic check charts, commercially produced tests, analytic and primary trait scales, cloze procedures, and curriculum-based assessments are variously used.

Provision for spelling involves skills or content, multi-sensory aspects, and Directed Spelling Thinking Activity, and target words. Grammar is conveyed using direct teaching/modelling, verbal practice, written practice, group and individual work, and encompassing the learner's own writing. Teaching and support for punctuation and capitalisation is systematic, based on assessments, and shaped to the requirements of individual learners. It combines explicit teaching with opportunities for application. Provision for writing composition includes developing self-regulation strategies, reducing task demands, frameworks for writing, writing for a purpose, and teaching reading and writing together. All these aspects of provisions inform curriculum and assessment, pedagogy, resources, and organisation. Therapeutic aspects relating to written expression are discussed Chapter 5, concerning developmental co-ordination disorder.

References

AdLit.org (2008) *Directed Reading Thinking Activity*. AdLit.org.

American Psychiatric Association (2013) *Diagnostic and Statistical Manual of Mental Disorders Fifth Edition (DSM-5)*. Washington DC, APA.

Berninger, V. W. (2009) 'Assessing and intervening with children with written language disorders' in Miller, D. (Ed.) *Best Practices in School Neuropsychology*. New York, Wiley (pp. 507–520).

Education Publishing Services. *SpellWell*. www.epsbooks.com.

Egan, L. H. (2001) *Noun Hounds and Other Great Grammar Games*. Scholastic. www.scolastic.com.

Fortes, I. S., Paula, C. S., Oliveira, M. C., Bordin, I. A., Mari, J. de J., and Rohde, L. A. (2016) 'A cross-sectional study to assess the prevalence of DSM-5 specific learning disorders in representative school samples from the second to sixth grade in Brazil'. *European Child and Adolescent Psychiatry* 25, pp. 195–207.

Graham, S. and Harris, K. R. (2011) 'Writing and students with disabilities' in Kauffman, J. M. and Hallahan, D. P. (Eds.) *Handbook of Special Education*. New York and London, Routledge.

Great Source. *Great Source Write Traits®*. www.greatsource.com.

Harris, K. R., Graham, S. and Mason, L. (2006) 'Improving the writing, knowledge and motivation of struggling young writers: Effects of self-regulated strategy development with and without peer support'. *American Educational Research Journal* 43, 295–340.

Project Read. *Language Circle/Project Read Written Expression Curriculum*. www.projectread.com.

Mason, L. H., Snyder, K. H., Sukhram, D. P., and Kedem, Y. (2006) 'TWA +PLANS strategies for expository reading and writing: Effects for nine fourth-grade students'. *Exceptional Children* 73, 69–89.

Mather. N., Wendling, B. J., and Roberts, R. (2009) *Writing Assessment and Instruction for Students with Learning Disabilities*. 2nd edition. San Francisco, CA, Jossey-Bass/John Wiley.

Pollock, J., Waller, E., and Pollitt, R. (2004) *Day-to-Day Dyslexia in the Classroom*. 2nd edition. London, Routledge Falmer.

Pugh, K., Frost, S., Sandak, R., Gillis, M., Moore, D., Jenner, A., and Menci, E. (2006) 'What does reading have to tell us about writing? Preliminary questions and methodological challenges in examining the neurobiological foundations of writing and writing disabilities' in McArthur, C., Graham, S., and Fitzgerald, J. (Eds.) *Handbook of Writing Research* (pp. 433–448. New York, Guilford.

Robertson, G. S. and Wilkinson, G. S. (2017) *Wide Range Achievement Test (WRAT5)*. 5th edition. Pearson.

Scholastic. *Noun Hounds and Other Great Grammar Games.* www.scolastic.com.

Schoolhouse Rock! *Grammar Rock.* www.schoolhouserock.com.

Sopris West. *Spellography.* www.sopriswest.com.

Chapter 4

Impairment in mathematics

Introduction

After mentioning the complex nature of mathematics, I discuss 'number sense' as a foundation for mathematical understanding and skill. Definitions of impairment in mathematics, specific disorder of arithmetical skills, and dyscalculia are examined. I indicate the prevalence of impairment in mathematics and its co-occurrence with other disorders. Possible physiological and emotional causal factors relating to mathematics impairment are discussed. I examine identification and assessment through commercially available tests, early identification based on observation of apparent difficulties, and assessment based on an individual's response to intervention.

Concerning provision, the chapter discusses the curriculum and related assessment. Examples of pedagogy are examined: explicit teaching and practice of number sense, the progress from concrete experience to symbolic representations and basic number facts, developing understanding of mathematics language, learning from everyday experiences of mathematics, using computer for mathematics learning, and reducing mathematics anxiety.

Regarding resources, I consider concrete materials like rods and blocks, adapted equipment, and computer software. Concerning therapy, counselling for severe mathematics anxiety is discussed. Group organisation is examined including opportunities for learners to respond and to talk about their thinking, and small group and paired discussions.

The importance of mathematics and mathematics learning

Mathematics, like literacy, permeates modern society, understanding of at least basic numeracy being a requirement of everyday life. Dealing

DOI: 10.4324/9781003177975-4

with household bills, bank accounts, shopping (on-line or in stores), and eating out, are among the many examples. In occupations too there are varying degrees of demand for an understanding of mathematics. As well as jobs where a high degree of mathematics understanding is essential, such as engineering or computing, many other occupations from building and carpentry to shop keeping and working on public transport require good mathematical skills.

Learners are likely to be aware of the importance of mathematics. But it is a real educational skill to convey the wonder and excitement of it. Still harder is the task of encouraging and building the skills and confidence of learners who dislike mathematics and who feel anxious in even approaching it.

The nature of mathematics

Shelves of books have been written about what mathematics is, ranging from philosophical analyses to practical guides. But for current purposes, mathematics can be briefly defined as being an abstract area of knowledge concerning number, quantity, and space. Pure mathematics deals with these as abstract concepts. Applied mathematics is concerned more with the use of mathematics in other disciplines and areas such as physics, and engineering. Accepted fields of mathematics are arithmetic, algebra, geometry, and analysis and many further subdivisions are also used.

A foundation to understanding and skill in mathematics

In coming to understand and develop skill in mathematics, an important foundation is number sense. As we will see shortly problems with number sense is a feature of impairment in mathematics.

Number sense involves

- 'number concept, number combination – arithmetic facts, computing and place value',
- 'ways of representing and establishing relationships among numbers',
- 'visualising the relative magnitude of collections',
- 'estimating numerical outcomes and mastering arithmetic facts' and using them proficiently,
- 'flexibly using number relationships', and
- 'making sense of numerical information' in different contexts (Sharma, 2015, p. 277).

An aspect of number sense that develops early is subitising. If you are shown two clusters of items, you can see immediately when one cluster is significantly greater than another without counting. You are also able to see the number value of small clusters of items straight away. As number sense develops it becomes possible to represent and use a number in many ways influenced by context and purpose. You should be able fluently and easily to decompose and recompose numbers (break them down into their parts and put them together again such as 9 being 5 and 4, and 5 and 4 being 9) (Sharma, 2015, p. 277).

Proficiency in number sense helps in developing numeracy – the ability to carry out whole number operations correctly, consistently, fluently, and with understanding. Numeracy also involves being able to estimate and to calculate accurately and efficiently. A learner should be able to do this mentally and 'on paper' using various strategies and means of calculation (Sharma, 2015, p. 277).

Definitions relating to impairment in mathematics

Relevant definitions relate to impairment in mathematics, specific disorder of arithmetical skills, and dyscalculia.

Impairment in mathematics

A difficulty in understanding and learning mathematics, impairment in mathematics is not associated with general intellectual disability. Lower than typical mental ability does not explain the disorder and general ability may for example be within the typical range while mathematics is below.

In the *Diagnostic and Statistical Manual Fifth Edition (DSM-5)* (American Psychiatric Association, 2013, pp. 66–74) the impairment is a form of specific learning disorder which may involve combinations of impairment in reading, written expression, or mathematics. Broadly speaking, a specific learning disorder concerns 'difficulties learning and using academic skills'. Targeted interventions have been used to rectify these difficulties, but they have persisted. Specific learning disorder begins during school-age years and its indications are not better accounted for by other conditions or factors, such as intellectual disabilities or 'inadequate educational instruction'.

Impairment in mathematics concerns two broad difficulties. The first involves number sense, memorisation of arithmetic facts, and accurate and fluent calculation. An individual has 'a poor understanding of numbers, their magnitude, and relationships; counts on fingers to add single-digit numbers instead of recalling the math facts as peers do; gets lost in the midst of arithmetic computation and may switch procedures'

(Ibid., p. 67). The second area of difficulty concerns accurate mathematics reasoning, involving severe difficulties in 'applying mathematical concepts, facts, or procedures to solve quantitative problems' (Ibid., pp. 66–74).

Specific disorder of arithmetical skills

Relatedly, the specific disorder of arithmetical skills is described as 'a specific impairment'. Like mathematics impairment, this disorder is not explicable owing solely to general cognitive impairment (or inadequate schooling). It concerns 'mastery of basic computational skills of addition, subtraction, multiplication and division rather than of the more abstract skills involved in algebra, trigonometry, geometry or calculus' (World Health Organisation, 2010).

Dyscalculia

In England, 'dyscalculia', like dyslexia and dyspraxia, is seen as a 'specific learning difficulty' (Department for Education/Department of Health, 2014, paragraph 6.31). Dyscalculia relates to certain core deficits including importantly, 'poor number sense that affects the acquisition of the four basic operations – addition, subtraction, multiplication and division' and their application to solving word problems (Emerson, 2015, p. 221).

A distinction is made between 'primary' and 'secondary' developmental dyscalculia. Showing itself in different ways in different people, the first arises from individual deficits – behavioural, cognitive, neuropsychological, and neuronal impacting on numeracy. 'Secondary' developmental dyscalculia refers to numerical/arithmetic dysfunctions caused by impairments not specifically relating to numeracy, for example, attention disorders which would be expected to impair performance more generally (Kaufmann et al., 2013).

Impairment in mathematics: Prevalence and co-occurrence with other disorders

Prevalence

Several factors make it hard to specify the prevalence of impairment in mathematics. Given that definitions of mathematics and arithmetic are complex and excite debate, so impairment in mathematics is difficult to pin down. Relatedly, the severity threshold at which mathematics difficulties become an impairment is not universally agreed. Adding to the confusion is overlap between aspects of specific learning disorder (reading, writing, mathematics).

All this leads to rather wide estimates of prevalence for specific learning disorder 'across the academic domains of reading, writing and mathematics' of 5% to 15% as proposed by *DSM-5* (American Psychiatric Association, 2013, p. 70). Estimates of the prevalence of 'dyscalculia' are 6.5% or more (Butterworth, 2010). Prevalence of 'developmental dyscalculia' is 'about 5 to 7%' (Zhou and Cheng (2015, p. 78).

Co-occurrence of impairment in mathematics with other disorders

The way specific learning disorders are understood suggests a likely overlap in the different expressions of the disorders in reading, writing, and mathematics, as well as co-ordination. Other disorders or difficulties also occur along with impairment in mathematics.

Unsurprisingly, individuals with deficits in arithmetic often also have reading disorder (Landerl and Moll, 2010). Deficits in visuo-spatial working memory occur together with arithmetic difficulties (Schuchardt, Maehler, and Hasselhorn, 2008). Attention deficits co-occur with mathematics problems (Czamara et al., 2013).

Because their presence can have implications for provision, it is important to be aware of the possibility of co-occurring disorders or difficulties. An individual who has dyscalculia with no other disorders may be able to use compensatory mechanisms when doing arithmetic. However, if learners have other accompanying disorders or difficulties, compensation mechanisms may not be so easy, suggesting that different approaches could be necessary for learning to be effective (Landerl, 2015, p. 121).

Causal factors

Although it may sound pedantic even evasive, the phrase 'causal factors' (rather than just 'causes') conveys the notion that there are no known direct and unequivocal causes of mathematics disorder. Rather there are a range of factors that may in combinations lead to an increased likelihood of an individual experiencing mathematics disorder.

Developmental dyscalculia may be caused by differences in functioning and/or structure in brain areas associated with mathematics. But disagreement emerges about the existence of such neural correlates (Bugden and Ansari, 2015) and if they do exist, whether they explain the disorder (Cowan, 2015, p. 1028).

Studies have been made of numerical magnitude processing and of arithmetic. One reason why these are important is because some research suggests that individual differences in mathematics achievement relate to basic number processing skills such as the ability to process numerical magnitudes (Orrantiaa et al., 2018)

For example, neuroimaging studies of children with developmental dyscalculia have examined the parietal cortex of the brain. Associated with (among other functions) mathematical problem solving, the parietal cortex is the surface of the parietal lobe. Research has shown abnormalities in the structure and functioning of this part of the brain (Bugden and Ansari, 2015, p. 37).

Studies have been made of the intra-parietal sulcus (an area of the brain which processes mathematics). These include research involving people with Turner's syndrome, children with foetal alcohol syndrome, and those with low birth weight. In these groups there is a higher than typical occurrence of dyscalculia and individuals tend to show less brain activity in the intra-parietal sulcus. Dehaene (2011) gives an overview of neurological evidence.

Anxiety can exacerbate difficulties with mathematics. Mathematics anxiety is a 'negative and potentially impairing emotional reaction to mathematics' (Moore, McAuley, Allred, and Ashcraft, 2015). Such a reaction can be precipitated by fears of failure or of appearing stupid which may relate to a learner's experience of mathematics or perceptions of it.

Identification and assessment

In identifying impairment in mathematics, assessors bear in mind its definition and its characteristic difficulties such as set out, for example, in *DSM-5* criteria (American Psychiatric Association, 2013, pp. 66–74). Forms of assessment include commercially available tests, early identification, and assessment based on an individual's response to intervention.

Commercial assessments

Examining underlying neurodevelopmental processes supporting mathematics skills, the *Feifer Assessment of Mathematics* (Feifer, 2016) covers the age range from pre-Kindergarten to college. It includes a short (15 minute) screening form. As well as a total index score, the assessment gives three index scores (Verbal, Procedural, and Semantic) each intended to represent a subtype of dyscalculia. A Verbal Index score concerns automatic fact retrieval and linguistic components of mathematics, while the Procedural Index score concerns ability to count, order, and sequence numbers or mathematical procedures. Finally, the Semantic Index score measures visual-spatial and conceptual components (e.g., magnitude representation, patterns and relationships, higher level maths problems solving, and number sense).

Comprising a book and copiable assessment sheets used for investigating numeracy abilities, *The Dyscalculia Assessment* (Emerson and Babtie, 2013) provides evidence of a learner's number sense and ability to calculate. This informs a personalised teaching programme for individual learners or small groups having difficulties with numbers. In England, it is used mainly with children aged 5 to 11, but is adaptable for older learners.

The *Beery Tests of Motor and Non-Motor Skills* (Beery, Beery, and Buktenika, 2010) recognises that non-verbal deficits such as spatial perception may influence mathematics performance. This may relate to non-motor dyspraxic effects in interpreting visually presented material (Emerson, 2015, p. 221).

Early identification

Early identification applies to spotting difficulties in young children before the problems are compounded by later failure and frustration. It also concerns recognising indications of difficulties at any age that may impair difficulties with mathematics learning.

Consequently, it is important to understand factors supporting early mathematics development even prior to formal instruction, to try to develop a framework for assessing young children's mathematical abilities. Core number deficits for instance have been identified in 'non-symbolic approximate magnitude and/or small quantity representation' (Reeve and Gray, 2015, p. 44). An aspect of this is subitising. Other factors that may support symbolic mathematics development and contribute to identifying potential difficulties early are

- the role of language,
- everyday mathematics experiences,
- general cognitive functions, and
- a learner's ability to attend to number events in the environment (Ibid.).

Relatedly, 'warning signs' of dyscalculia are suggested:

- poor number sense;
- slow responses;
- difficulties with mathematics language;

- difficulty with memory for mathematics facts and procedures;
- difficulties with sequences; and
- difficulties with position and spatial organisation (Hannell, 2013, pp. 13–14).

Response to intervention assessment

A student may not make expected progress in mathematics, seemingly owing to problems with mathematics learning rather than another cause, such as illness, leading to missed education. In these circumstances, further investigations can be made.

As interventions are tried relating to the difficulties identified, what is taught and how it is taught are gradually modified. Essentially, this is a diagnostic 'response to intervention'.

Provision

Having different emphases, views of impairment in mathematics may have different foci. Some concentrate on core deficits. Others emphasise features of the disorder associated with impairment of reading (e.g., difficulties with phonological representations, auditory processing, and auditory perception). Yet others look to features associated with developmental co-ordination disorder such as visuo-spatial problems.

Spatial position, length, area, weight, shape, and volume have numerical aspects. Our focus is looking at provision in number. We also look at features such as co-ordination difficulties that may further hinder mathematics learning and discuss approaches that can help learners with impairment in mathematics.

Curriculum and assessment

Curriculum

A plan or programme of what is to be taught and learned, a curriculum can apply to various settings. Included are schools, tuition centres, a student's home (where programmes are taught by parents and others), and centres/clinics specialising in provision for specific learning difficulties.

For learners with impairment in mathematics, attainment in aspects of mathematics will be lower than that of others of the same age. Curriculum planning will therefore start from lower levels in mathematics (or parts of it). In a school or a tuition centre for example, where various areas of learning are taught, staff will identify areas where mathematics is a major component, such as various sciences. In these sessions, mathematics learning may be supported by pre-teaching the skills to be used, follow-up teaching to ensure understanding, and extra staff support for the learner.

In larger settings such as schools, curriculum content may reflect attainment levels that are lower than is typical for a learner's age but taught in age-appropriate ways ensuring that learners are engaged. Functional, everyday mathematics where the purpose and relevance of learning is made clear can motivate struggling learners. In planning mathematics in all aspects, educators should ensure that learning begins with concrete, practical examples, and experience before moving on to more abstract approaches.

Assessment

As well as the assessment involved in identification and assessment of mathematics disorder, curriculum-related assessment also occurs as the content of mathematics is taught.

Ongoing assessment while teaching is taking place does not just establish whether an answer to any problem is correct. It also takes account of the processes used by the learner to engage with the mathematics involved. The teacher will ask learners to explain their process of working out so that any misunderstandings come to light. Once any errors in understanding and the processes involved are recognised and put right, the solution to the problem tends to fall into place. This is often done with the teacher and learner sitting together. Simply marking a calculation as incorrect is useless to the learner if the reasons for a mistake are not identified and remedied. If group work is taken away to be 'marked', the teachers written comments will either ask the learner to speak with the teacher or will be detailed enough to explain the error and how it can be put right. Showing the learner how to improve is the best evaluative marking, which cannot be done unless the teacher knows why a mistake was made.

Consider reasons why a learner may have difficulties with place value.

- They may be confused because in a number line (1, 2, 3 …), numbers to the left are progressively smaller in value. Yet with digits, the value to the left is bigger in the sense that it represents tens, hundreds, etc. (e.g., in '24' the '2' on the left represents '20').
- Numbers may be misread so that the correct information is not used.
- Numbers may be written incorrectly, concealing that the learner may know the correct answer to the calculation.
- The student may not understand place value because of difficulties with the language used.

To rectify any mistakes relating to place value the teacher must ask the learner to explain their working out, revealing the exact misunderstanding so the best remedy can be determined. For further examples of types of errors and possible teacher responses see Hannell (2013, p. 31).

Pedagogy

Under pedagogy, we examine

- explicit teaching and practice of number sense,
- progressing from concrete experience to symbolic representations and basic number facts,
- developing understanding of mathematics language,
- using everyday experiences of mathematics,
- using computer for mathematics learning, and
- reducing mathematics anxiety.

Explicit teaching and practice of number sense

As Hannell (2013, p. 49) states, to properly understand the number system, learners must

- 'understand the number line and how numbers are positioned on it;
- have a strong sense of the order of magnitude of numbers;
- understand the relationship that numbers have with each other;
- count accurately and apply the skill of counting flexibly;
- understand how to use the base ten system in counting;
- understand place value in written numbers;
- understand the composition and decomposition of numbers'.

Learners with dyscalculia (compared with others of similar intelligence) need extra practice in many areas: more activities to help develop intuitive number sense; extra intensive, explicit teaching about the number system and extensive practice using it; plenty of time to acquire the basics; and concrete experience with large and small numbers (Ibid., p. 48, paraphrased).

Part of developing number sense is being able to form and automatically access the spatial representation of numbers (Kucian et al., 2011). This involves understanding the location of numbers relative to one another. Confident mathematical reasoning emerges from just 'knowing' how numbers are arranged in order of size and starting from this knowledge.

Helping learners begin to see how numbers relate, a physical number line shows that the differences between adjacent numbers is the same. The difference as represented by the spatial distance between 5 and 6 is the same as that between 7 and 8. Educators can teach understanding of the number line through activities including board games and playground pursuits. Given individual number cards, students can be asked to lay them in numerical order. In mental exercises, the teacher can ask student which number comes before or after a specified one. Learners can be shown the patterns of number sequences for example that the numbers from 20 to 30 echo the numbers from 1 to 10 in their repeated sequence of units. Hannell (2013, pp. 53–55) gives further examples.

If confused by simultaneously touching an item and counting, a student can be given tasks involving touching and naming items. These might be a sequence of coloured objects touched and named in correct order, such as 'red, blue, green, black, red, red'. This gets the learner to automatically touch and talk. After this is consolidated the learner might name items by numbers, 'one, two, three', perhaps picking up each item as it is counted. They might then count without touching. Next comes extensive practice of counting in a wide range of situations and using the skill in many practical real-life situations (Hannell, 2013, p. 57–58).

Longer term, moving from understanding number to basic calculation involves various skills and levels of understanding. It is important that the learner recognises and understands number patterns, such as patterns of twos or tens. Place value must be taught. Number composition and decomposition needs to be familiar to the student. Operations of addition, subtraction, multiplication, and division are directly taught.

Throughout, practical examples are used where possible, the learner is explicitly taught and given plenty of practice and opportunities to apply the new learning, and misunderstandings are detected early and corrected. Hannell (2013) provides examples of activities supporting this development. Such approaches are used more intensively for those experiencing severe difficulties in mathematics (scoring in the lowest 5%).

One such intervention is *Mathematics Recovery* (e.g., Wright, Stanger, Stafford, and Martland, 2014), which has several elements. These include ones aimed at students with difficulties emphasising methods of counting and number representation, as well as elements including other aspects of arithmetic. Following an in-depth initial assessment, the intensive programme involves a daily half hour of individualised intervention, delivered by people having received 60 hours of training.

Number Count, another intensive intervention (Dunn, Mathews, and Dowrick, 2011) also involves a thorough initial diagnostic assessment and half an hour individualised intervention per day delivered by people with Master's level training.

Progressing from concrete experience to symbolic representations and basic number facts

In teaching and learning mathematics, researchers have proposed a concrete–semi-concrete-abstract teaching sequence. Teaching first uses concrete representations (manipulatives) to represent concepts, followed by semi-concrete representations like tally marks or pictures, then abstract representation involving symbols (Bryant, Bryant, Shin, and Pfannenstiel, 2015, p. 251).

For learners with poor number sense who use ones-based counting strategies, concrete manipulatives can be used that students can see, touch, move, and talk about (Emerson, 2015, pp. 223–225). Initially, discrete materials are used like blocks, counters, or strings of beads. Teachers can use a ten-row Slavonic abacus with ten beads on each row, five of one colour and five of another. This helps the learner recognise a group of five beads, being the same colour. It aids counting on from five if there are say seven beads in a row (because five is easy to recognise as a group). When the learner is experienced using three-dimensional items, the items can be represented two-dimensionally by drawings, perhaps done by the learner.

Later, 'continuous material' is used such as Cuisenaire rods (physical aids using size and colour to help learners better understand aspects of mathematics). Numbers from 1 to 10 are represented by different length rods. Counting objects in lines of ten, students talk about what they see to reinforce the tens-based character of the number system. Items can be arranged in lines of ten on number tracks to emphasise the sense of items in groups of ten. Similarly, dot arrangements up to ten help familiarise learners with the patterns. Learners place the patterns in order according to the counting sequence while developing a quantitative awareness of the numbers relative to each other (Emerson, 2015, p. 223).

As learners comprehend how numbers are decomposed and composed (10 can be separated into 6 and 4; while 6 and 4 can be put together to make 10) they can use this understanding to help with number operations.

Certain approaches to number operations can help children with 'learning difficulties' to acquire mathematics skills (Hamak, Astilla, and Preclaro, 2015). To help retrieve number facts, learners are taught to break down larger quantities into manageable chunks. Helping develop learners' ability to visualise numbers, concrete materials like connectable blocks are used. They enable students to break quantities down and assist mental mathematical activities.

Breaking down quantities into manageable values helps learners having difficulties retrieving mathematical facts from memory. A learner may know the number bonds of 10 but may initially struggle with the task '9 + 8 ='. The 8 can be broken down into 1 and 7. The 1 can then be added to the 9 to make 10, given that this is a basic number fact that the learner already knows. The remaining 7 is then added to the ten to make 17.

Relatedly teachers can help learners recognise when, in linear addition sums, they can group numbers together to use already known mathematics facts. Consider the following:

$$5 + 6 + 9 + 8 + 4 + 2 + 1$$

Learners can group together the 9 and 1 to make 10, the 8 and 2 to make 10, and the 6 and 4 to make 10. They will see that this makes 30. They then add to this the 5 that has not been paired. This can be initially done using movable number tiles enabling the learner to pair them more easily (Hamak, Astilla, and Preclaro, 2015, pp. 210–213).

Developing understanding of mathematical language

Aspects of mathematical language are

- developing and using mathematical language itself,
- mathematical stories, and
- mathematics word problems.

Learners can *develop and use mathematical language* through direct instruction in mathematical terminology (Hamak, Astilla, and Preclaro, 2015). Words which are commonly used in other circumstances, but have a specific mathematical meaning, are taught, such as 'even', 'odd', and 'table'. Words commonly seen in mathematics are also taught as they arise, for example, 'circumference', 'area', and 'radius'.

Developing such language is linked with concrete examples and hands-on experience. Once the concept (say, 'circumference') is grasped then picture cards can be used to remind learners of the word and its meaning. By initiating talk about the concept and encouraging learners to use the words with increasing confidence, terminology is reinforced. This enables students to relate the new word and concept to what is already known.

Intended for 5-to-11-year-olds, *Talking Mathematics* (Education Works, 2011) can be used as a distinct approach, or integrated into current mathematics teaching. Typically taking about ten weeks to complete, the programme focuses on speaking and listening skills important when developing thinking strategies and tackling mathematical problems. Supporting the use of mathematical vocabulary and terminology, the intervention develops ability to reason, make generalisations, predict, and recognise patterns and relationships in mathematics. It is suitable for learners with some mathematical competence who need help in using and understanding mathematical language in the context of mathematics. The intervention provides guidance for teachers and classroom aides on how to use good mathematical language and questioning that the learners can 'model'.

Turning to *mathematical stories*, number stories can give learners a better understanding of word problems and how they are constructed. Making up and telling a story about '3' and '7', the student might tell of campers in a forest camp. There were seven at first. Three of them went out to explore and four were left. The learner then writes the different sums that could be made from the story such as '7 − 3 = 4'. This can build the confidence of learners struggling with terms such as 'subtract' and 'minus', helping them to develop the language necessary to picture and understand some principles in basic arithmetic.

Teachers can provide a framework by initially telling mathematical stories, which learners can elaborate before inventing stories of their own. Story-related props can be used to help the transitions between concrete and abstract representations of mathematical ideas (McGrath, 2015, p. 371).

As they develop mathematical language knowledge and skills, learners are taught how to deal with *mathematical word problems*, which involve more than might be apparent at first. Students must be able to

- understand the language and information to define the problem,
- construct a representation of the problem using the 'relevant elements and relations among quantities', and
- plan how to solve the problem, carry out the plans, and interpret the 'appropriateness and reasonableness' of the outcome relative to the original problem situation (Jitendra, Dupuis, and Lein, 2015, 357).

Teachers first introduce problems verbally rather than in writing, while students listen for key words in the sentence that will help an understanding of what is requested. They then translate the sentence into mathematical form and tackle it. First presenting simple sentences, teachers build up to more complicated ones to give a grounding for later written mathematical problems (Hamak, Astilla, and Preclaro, 2015, pp. 213–216).

Relatedly, teachers provide instruction making the common underlying problem structures explicit (Gersten et al., 2009). This enables learners to move beyond the surface features of the problem, like vocabulary, the way it is expressed, and any irrelevant information, and instead uncover the underlying mathematical structure, perhaps by drawing a diagram (Ibid., pp. 26–27).

Using everyday experiences of mathematics

When shown that mathematics is part of everyday life, learners can improve their number sense. This helps learners who are having memory difficulties by giving mathematics learning a relevance that aids memory. Everyday situations can convey that mathematics is part of the real world and not just of mathematics lessons.

To take a few examples relating to number, students can count books and items of equipment to be given out to a group to ensure there are sufficient amounts. In shopping, quantities of items can be checked. Calendars and sequences of days of the week can be confirmed. Introduced in many contexts and using many examples, understanding of the concept of 'more than' and 'less than' can be made secure and generalised.

Such experience of objects and number are helpful before using 'manipulatives', which involve abstraction that is hard for learners with impairment in mathematics to grasp. Manipulatives represent objects, making them one step removed from real experience.

Using computers for mathematics learning

Using animation or favourite characters to teach a mathematical skill, computers can be motivating. They enable tasks to be pitched accurately at a particular learner's level of skill and understanding, allowing well-structured individual work.

Harskamp (2015, p. 384) distinguishes two categories of software. The first is 'tutorials', which are suited to practicing knowledge and skills. These help educators allowing practice or re-teaching of mathematics by giving the learner demonstrations, explanations, and guided practice.

'Exploratory environments', the second category of software, encourage active learning through exploration and discovery. For example, hypermedia-based learning allows access to information through links within text, images, animation, audio, and video. Its non-linear nature and flexibility enable different learning needs to be accommodated. Also, computer simulations (including in computer games) can improve learning. They enable learners to simulate real-life situations in a programmed environment, when it might be too expensive or unsafe to experience the real-life equivalent (Harskamp, 2015, p. 384).

Reducing mathematics anxiety

A 'negative and potentially impairing emotional reaction to mathematics' (Moore, McAuley, Allred, and Ashcraft, 2015), mathematics anxiety diminishes achievement and career opportunities. Learners with mathematics anxiety tend get worse grades than peers in high school and college and are less likely to follow mathematics courses and degrees or take up mathematics-related careers (Ibid., p. 328). A learner may fear appearing incompetent in front of peers. Mathematics anxiety inhibits learning by essentially rerouting working memory resources towards emotional regulation centres of the brain (Ibid., p. 332).

This seems to correspond with perceptions that some learners become unusually anxious when expected to demonstrate competence in applying mathematical skills. Sometimes attention difficulties are exacerbated by stress and anxiety about doing mathematics.

By reassuring the learner and making mathematics enjoyable, perhaps using games, anxiety can be reduced, helping the learner to relax, and to concentrate and attend better. Where a student experiences high levels of anxiety about mathematics, individual tuition can help ensure early success and reduce the worry about getting the task wrong.

Temporarily minimising the learning challenge (Fuchs et al., 2008) builds the student's confidence by providing many foundational experiences of success. As an educator, you can give precise explanations to anticipate the problems that the learner will likely encounter. Where worries about mathematics are part of a more general, severe level of anxiety, counselling may be provided.

Resources

For learners with mathematics disorder, concrete materials are important in laying down a foundation to learning. Cuisenaire rods, Dienes MAB blocks, Stern's equipment and Unifix blocks are used in developing understanding of computation and other mathematical understanding. Equipment may be adapted. With linear measuring, a learner having difficulties with fine motor co-ordination may use a ruler with a small handle on the flat broad side.

Through exploration and discovery, computers can encourage active learning. Commercially available materials include *The Number Race* (www.thenumberrace.com) designed to improve number sense for those with dyscalculia particularly for ages 4 to 8 years. Another resource, *Bubble Reef* (www.sheppardsoftware.com) comprises 12 multimedia games involving basic number activities of counting, numeral recognition, sequencing, and simple operations. Set underwater, it involves various aquatic characters. *MathBase 1* (www.mathbase.co.uk) is UK software focusing on basic number concepts, which offers more advanced modules as the learner progresses. Using the familiar setting of an open-air market and day-to-day experiences to develop number sense, *To Market to Market* (www.learninginmotion.com) is US software package.

Therapy

Where a learner experiences severe mathematics anxiety, perhaps in the context of wider anxiety disorder, counselling may be provided.

Organisation

Explicit systematic instruction is helpful to learners with mathematics disorder and should offer opportunities for learners to respond and to talk through their thinking (Gersten et al., 2008; the Instructional Research Group, California, www.inresg.org). Therefore, classroom and group organisation that facilitates this should aid learning. If well focused, opportunities for small group discussions and for learners to speak with partners can be beneficial.

Conclusion

Mathematics is complex, suggesting that dealing with impairment in mathematics is likely to be challenging. Developing number sense is a foundation for mathematical understanding and skill. Definitions of impairment in mathematics, specific disorder of arithmetical skills, and dyscalculia differ in detail. Estimates of the prevalence of dyscalculia are 6.5% or more. Impairment in mathematics overlaps with disorders in reading, writing, and mathematics, as well as co-ordination. Deficits in visuo-spatial working memory occur together with arithmetic difficulties, and attention deficits co-occur with mathematics problems.

Some neuroimaging studies of children with developmental dyscalculia have shown abnormalities in the structure and functioning of the parietal cortex. In groups with Turner's syndrome, children with foetal alcohol syndrome, and those with low birth weight, dyscalculia is more frequent than typically, and there tends to be less brain activity in the intra-parietal sulcus. Mathematics anxiety can be precipitated by fear of failure, or of appearing stupid (both possibly relating to a learner's experience of mathematics or perceptions of it). Commercially available tests, early identification based on observation of apparent difficulties, and assessment based on an individual's response to intervention are used for identification and assessment.

For learners with impairment in mathematics, curriculum planning starts from lower levels in mathematics (or parts of it). In settings where various areas of learning are taught, including subjects where mathematics is a major component, mathematics learning may be supported. This can be by pre-teaching the skills to be used, follow-up teaching to ensure understanding, and extra staff support. Ongoing assessment during teaching takes account of the processes used by the learner to engage with mathematics.

Pedagogy includes explicit teaching and practice of number sense, concrete experience to symbolic representations, and basic number facts, developing understanding of mathematics language, using everyday experiences of mathematics, using computer for mathematics learning, and reducing mathematics anxiety. Concrete materials like rods and blocks, adapted equipment, and computer software are used. Counselling may be provided for severe mathematics anxiety. Learners are given opportunities to respond and to talk through their thinking and participate in small group and paired discussions.

Thinking points

You may wish to consider the relative effectiveness of approaches discussed in this chapter and how these approaches can be rationalised into comprehensive and coherent provision.

Key texts

Chin, S. (Ed.) (2017) *Routledge International Handbook for Dyscalculia and Mathematical Learning Difficulties*. London and New York, Routledge.

This book comprises articles from different countries outlining various aspects of mathematical learning difficulties and dyscalculia. These vary from comprehensive reviews to journal-type contributions presenting a single piece of research.

An example of an Internet site giving a brief overview of mathematics disorder is www.schwablearning.org/articles.

Resources

The Number Race (www.thenumberrace.com).
Bubble Reef (www.sheppardsoftware.com).
MathBase 1 (www.mathbase.co.uk).
To Market to Market (www.learninginmotion.com).

References

American Psychiatric Association (2013) *Diagnostic and Statistical Manual of Mental Disorders Fifth Edition (DSM-5)*. Washington DC, APA.

Beery, K. E., Beery, N. A., and Buktenika, N. A. (2010) *Beery Test of Visual Perception*. 6th edition. London, Pearson.

Bryant, D. P., Bryant, B. R., Shin, M., and Pfannenstiel, K. H. (2015) 'Learning disabilities: Mathematics characteristics and instructional exemplars' in Chin, S. (Ed.) *Routledge International Handbook for Dyscalculia and Mathematical Learning Difficulties*. London and New York, Routledge.

Budd, C. J. (2015) 'Promoting maths to the general public' in Cohen Kadosh, R. and Dowker, A. (Eds.) *The Oxford Handbook of Numerical Cognition* (Oxford Library of Psychology). Oxford, Oxford University Press (pp. 3–16).

Bugden, S. and Ansari, D. (2015) 'How can cognitive developmental neuroscience constrain our understanding of developmental dyscalculia?' in Chin, S. (Ed.) *Routledge International Handbook for Dyscalculia and Mathematical Learning Difficulties*. London and New York, Routledge (pp. 18–43).

Butterworth, B. (2003) *Dyscalculia Screener*. Swindon, NFER-Nelson.

Butterworth, B. (2010) 'Foundational numerical capacities and the origins of dyscalculia'. *Trends in Cognitive Sciences* 14, 12, 534–541.

Chin, S. (2012) *More Trouble with Maths*. London and New York, Routledge.

Chin, S. (Ed.) (2017) *Routledge International Handbook for Dyscalculia and Mathematical Learning Difficulties*. London and New York, Routledge.

Cowan, R. (2015) 'Education' in Cohen Kadosh, R. and Dowker, A. (Eds.) *The Oxford Handbook of Numerical Cognition* (Oxford Library of Psychology). Oxford, Oxford University Press (pp. 1021–1035).

Czamara, D., Tiesler, C. M. T., Kohlböck, G. et al. (2013) 'Children with ADHD symptoms have a higher risk for reading, spelling and math difficulties in the GINIplus and LISAplus cohort studies'. *PLOS ONE* 85, 5, e63859.

Dehaene, S. (2011) *The Number Sense: How the Mind Creates Mathematics* New York, Oxford University Press.

Department for Education/Department of Health (2014) *Special Educational Needs and Disability Code of Practice: 0 To 25 Years – Statutory Guidance for Organisations Who Work with and Support Children and Young People with Special Educational Needs and Disabilities*. London, DfE/DoH (June 2014).

Dunn, S., Mathews, L., and Dowrick, N. (2011) 'Numbers count: Developing a national approach to intervention' in Thompson, I. (Ed.) *Issues in Teaching Numeracy in Primary Schools*. Maidenhead, Open University Press (pp. 224–234).

Education Works (2011) *Talking Mathematics.* www.educationworks.org.uk.

Emerson, J. (2015) 'The enigma of dyscalculia' in Chin, S. (Ed.) *Routledge International Handbook for Dyscalculia and Mathematical Learning Difficulties.* London and New York, Routledge (pp. 217–227).

Emerson, J. and Babtie, P. (2013) *The Dyscalculia Assessment.* 2nd edition. London, Bloomsbury.

Feifer, S. G. (2016) *Feifer Assessment of Mathematics.* Psychological Assessment Resources.

Fuchs, L. S., Fuchs, D. F., Powell, S., et al. (2008) 'Inclusive intervention for students with mathematics disabilities: Seven principles of effective practice'. *Learning Disability Quarterly* 31, 2, 79–92.

Gersten, R., Chard, D. C., Jayanthi, M., Baker, S. K., Morphy, P., and Flojo, J. (2008) *Mathematics Instruction for Students with Learning Disabilities or Difficulties Learning Mathematics: A Synthesis of the Intervention Research.* Portsmouth, NH: RCM Research Corporation, Center on Instruction.

Gersten, R., Beckmann, S., Clarke, B.et al. (2009) *Assisting Students Struggling with Mathematics: Response to Intervention (RtI) for Elementary and Middle Schools* (NCEE 2009–4060). Washington, DC, National Centre for Education Evaluation and Regional Assistance, Institute of Education Sciences, U S Department of Education.

Hamak, S., Astilla, J., and Preclaro, H. R. (2015) 'The acquisition of mathematics skills of Filipino children with learning difficulties: Issues and challenges' in Chin, S. (Ed) *The Routledge International Handbook of Dyscalculia and Mathematical Learning Difficulties.* London, Routledge (pp. 203–216).

Hannell, G. (2013) *Dyscalculia: Action Plans for Successful Learning in Mathematics.* London, Routledge.

Harskamp, E. (2015) 'The effects of computer technology on primary school students' mathematics achievement' in Chin, S. (Ed.) *Routledge International Handbook for Dyscalculia and Mathematical Learning Difficulties.* London and New York, Routledge.

Jitendra, A. K., Dupuis, D. N., and Lein, A. E. (2015) 'Promoting word problem solving performance among students with mathematical difficulties: The role of strategy instruction that primes the problem structure' in Chin, S. (Ed.) *Routledge International Handbook for Dyscalculia and Mathematical Learning Difficulties.* London and New York, Routledge.

Kaufmann, L., Mazzocco, M. M., Dowker, A.et al. (2013) 'Dyscalculia from a developmental and differential perspective'. *Frontiers in Psychology* 4, 516.

Kucian, K., Grond, U., Rotzer, S.et al. (2011) 'Mental number line training in children with developmental dyscalculia'. *NeuroImage* 57, 782–795.

Landerl, K. (2015) 'How specific is the specific disorder of arithmetic skills?' in Chin, S. (Ed.) *Routledge International Handbook for Dyscalculia and Mathematical Learning Difficulties.* London and New York, Routledge (pp. 115–124).

Landerl, K. and Moll, K. (2010) 'Comorbidity of learning disorders: Prevalence and familial transmission'. *Journal of Clinical Child Psychology and Psychiatry* 51, 287–294.

McGrath, C. (2015) 'Mathematical storyteller kings and queens: An alternative pedagogical choice to facilitate mathematical thinking and understand children's mathematical capabilities' in Chin, S. (Ed.) *Routledge International Handbook for Dyscalculia and Mathematical Learning Difficulties*. London and New York, Routledge.

Moore, A. M., McAuley, A. J., Allred, G. A., and Ashcraft, M. H. (2015) 'Mathematics anxiety, working memory, and mathematical performance: The triple task effect and the affective drop in performance' in Chin, S. (Ed.) *Routledge International Handbook for Dyscalculia and Mathematical Learning Difficulties*. London and New York, Routledge.

Orrantiaa, J., Romualdoa, S. S., Sáncheza, R., Matillaa, L., Múñez, D., and Verschaffelc, L. (June, 2018) 'Numerical magnitude processing and mathematics achievement'. *Revista de Educación*.

Reeve, R. A. and Gray, S. (2015) 'Number difficulties in young children' in Chin, S. (Ed.) *Routledge International Handbook for Dyscalculia and Mathematical Learning Difficulties*. London and New York, Routledge (pp. 44–59).

Schuchardt, K., Maehler, C., and Hasselhorn, M. (2008) 'Working memory in children with specific learning disorders'. *Journal of Learning Disabilities* 41, 514–523.

Sharma, M. C. (2015) 'Numbersense: A window into dyscalculia and other mathematics difficulties' in Chin, S. (Ed.) *Routledge International Handbook for Dyscalculia and Mathematical Learning Difficulties*. London and New York, Routledge (pp. 277–291).

World Health Organisation (2010) 'F81.2 Specific disorder of arithmetical skills' in *The ICD-10 Classification of Mental and Behavioural Disorders*. Geneva, WHO.

Wright, R. J., Stanger, G., Stafford, A. K. and Martland, J. (2014) *Teaching Number in the Classroom with 4 to 8 Year Olds (Math Recovery)*. London, Sage.

Zhou, X. and Cheng, D. (2015) 'When and why numerosity processing is associated with developmental dyscalculia' in Chin, S. (Ed.) *Routledge International Handbook for Dyscalculia and Mathematical Learning Difficulties*. London and New York, Routledge (pp. 78–89).

Chapter 5

Developmental co-ordination disorder

Introduction

In this chapter, I discuss definitions of developmental co-ordination disorder (DCD) (with its origins in notions of clumsiness), understandings of DCD and dyspraxia, and types of motor difficulties. I consider the pervasive nature of DCD, its prevalence and co-occurrence with other disorders. Possible genetic and neurological causal factors are touched on. Considering identification and assessment the chapter looks at screening tests, implications for tests at different ages, standardised tests, multi-professional assessments, and eligibility for special provision.

I examine curriculum and related assessment. Pedagogy is discussed in relation to general classroom approaches, specific skills training, and accommodations to increase student participation. Also examined is pedagogy in relation to the important areas of physical education, personal and social education, and handwriting. I look at resources with reference to special and adapted equipment, and the different uses regular resources. Physical therapy is considered relative to two interventions Neuromotor Task Training and Cognitive Orientation to Daily Occupational Performance. I discuss organisation including the layout of furniture and equipment in rooms.

Definitions

DCD is more than clumsiness

Formerly, it was common to use the expression 'clumsy child syndrome' for what is now called developmental co-ordination disorder (DCD). Indeed, a recent succinct description of DCD is that it refers to children, 'whose clumsiness has no known medical cause' and 'whose everyday social and academic functioning is significantly impaired' (Cairney, 2015, pp. 5–6).

DOI: 10.4324/9781003177975-5

While the focus on clumsiness may convey a common feature of the condition or at least a possible subtype, it misses some subtle implications which are more complex than just the idea of clumsiness suggests. Consequences of DCD can include an impact on socialisation, physical health and fitness, and mental well-being.

Developmental co-ordination disorder and dyspraxia

Widely used diagnostic guidance (American Psychiatric Association, 2013) defines DCD as a condition in which, acquiring and carrying out co-ordinated motor skills is 'substantially below that expected'. Such expectations are based on the person's chronological age and previous opportunities to learn and use the skills in question. Difficulties show themselves as 'clumsiness' and 'slowness and inaccuracy of performance of motor skills' (Ibid., p. 74).

Furthermore, the motor skills deficit 'significantly and persistently interferes with activities of daily living appropriate to chronological age'. It inhibits 'academic/school productivity, prevocational and vocational activities, leisure and play' (Ibid., p. 74). Symptoms start in the 'early developmental period'.

Care is taken to avoid confusing DCD with the effects of other conditions. Broad intellectual disability can lead to poor and uncoordinated movement, as can visual impairment. Other conditions affect movement because of neurological conditions. A neurological disorder of movement, affecting muscle co-ordination, and balance and impairing walking, ataxia, for example, is caused by damage to the cerebellum a part of the brain controlling muscle co-ordination. To avoid confusion with such conditions, criteria for DCD state that evident deficits in motor skills are not better explained by 'intellectual disability ... or visual impairment'. Nor are they attributable to 'a neurological condition affecting movement' (Ibid.).

Some countries still use the term 'dyspraxia' (from the Greek for 'difficulty in doing'). It is sometimes regarded as a subtype of DCD. For example, the Dyspraxia Foundation describes it as 'a form of developmental disorder' which affects 'fine and/or gross motor coordination' (www.dyspraxiafoundation.org.uk/about-dyspraxia).

Definitions of dyspraxia tend to emphasise the planning and organisation of movement.

Types of motor problems

Helping to provide a fuller picture of the condition, as well as definitions of DCD there are descriptions of motor problems experienced with the condition. Such descriptions convey the variable nature of DCD.

Problems with fine motor control make activities involving manipulation with the fingers and hands exceedingly difficult, as illustrated by dressing, eating with cutlery, writing, and drawing, and using scissors. Individuals may experience difficulties with gross motor movements when finding a route around furniture, participating in sports, and sitting on a chair safely. Motor co-ordination difficulties may be behind secondary problems such as limited participation in activities, poor physical health, and frustration-led disruptive behaviour (Cairney, 2015, pp. 10–11).

Geuze (2005) identified three types of problems experienced by learners with DCD:

- poor postural control or difficulties with static and dynamic balance;
- poor sensorimotor co-ordination covering motor planning, timing, anticipating, and using 'feedback' to respond to environmental changes; and
- problems with motor learning involving learning new skills, adapting to changes, and automatisation (focusing on a task while carrying out other movements required for co-ordinated action with little or no conscious attention).

Compared with children of the same age, children with DCD tend to be much slower in processing visuospatial information.

Implications of developmental co-ordination disorder

Implications of DCD are many. DCD can limit participation in physical pursuits and in social activities at work, at school, at home, and in the community. Reduced involvement in activities in turn affects the development of skills and of physical and emotional well-being (Engel-Yeger, 2015, pp. 47–48). Restrictions in play and leisure activities can limit opportunities to develop socially and in other ways (Cairney, 2015, p. 62). Leading to reduced physical activity, low motor competence can affecting health, especially cardiovascular health (Ibid.).

Studies of interactions between DCD and its social and emotional consequences suggest possible relationships with anxiety, depression, self-perception, and social skills (Piek and Rigoli, 2015, p. 126).

Missiuna, Polatajko, and Pollock (2015) convincingly state that

> Twenty-five years of research has produced compelling evidence that the motor problems of children with DCD are lifelong … and that these motor difficulties are strongly associated with the subsequent development of physical and mental health difficulties,

including decreased physical fitness ... obesity ... anxiety ... depression ... low self-esteem ... and also academic failure ....

(Ibid., pp. 215–216)

Prevalence and co-occurrence with other disorders

Prevalence of DCD

In children aged 5 to 11 years, the prevalence of DCD is 5% to 6%. A male:female ratio ranging from 2:1 to 7:1 is found (American Psychiatric Association, 2013, p. 75). However, population-based studies of children with DCD suggest that more equal numbers of boys and girls may be affected (Edwards et al., 2011).

Co-occurrence of DCD with other disorders

Co-occurrence of DCD with other conditions can be high. Regarding attention deficit hyperactivity disorder, co-occurrence is about 50%. Other conditions commonly co-occurring with DCD are speech and language disorder, specific learning disorder, autism spectrum disorder, and disruptive and emotional behaviour problems.

Clusters may occur with severe reading impairment, handwriting difficulties, and fine motor problems. Impaired movement control and motor planning is another cluster (American Psychiatric Association, 2013, p. 77).

Causal factors

We do not yet understand the aetiology of DCD fully. Some researchers have proposed a possible genetic element (Gaines et al., 2008). Originating early in life, the condition may develop while the child is in the womb or soon after birth. DCD may result from damage as the brain is developing when neural pathways governing motor co-ordination and control are forming. Preterm birth appears to be a risk factor (Cairney, 2015, p. 15).

While complex, neurological evidence is beginning to point to possible causal factors. Brain imaging studies suggest that DCD may be associated with dysfunction of the parietal lobes and the cerebellum, a part of the brain involved in motor co-ordination and postural control (Zwicker, Missiuna, Harris, and Boyd, 2010a; Zwicker, Missiuna, Harris, and Boyd, 2010b). In children with DCD, neurological mechanisms involved in predicting motor control may be compromised. Also, there are deficits in executive control (Wilson, 2015, p. 157).

Identification and assessment

We consider identification and assessment of DCD in relation to

- screening tests,
- implications for tests at different ages,
- standardised tests,
- multi-professional assessments, and
- eligibility for special provision.

Screening tests

Given the potential for secondary difficulties to develop, early identification of DCD is important. However, there are some reservations about the sensitivity of screening tests in identifying DCD and motor difficulties more generally. Despite these limitations, screening questionnaires can provide important information about functional motor abilities of children at home and at school (Schoemaker and Wilson, 2015, pp 169–191).

Implications of assessments at different ages

In carrying out an assessment, the assessor needs to be aware of possible characteristics of the condition at different ages and periods of development. Children of 4 or 5 years old with DCD may find it harder than peers to go up and down stairs. They may learn to use the toilet independently much later than other children and have difficulty handling toys and performing tasks requiring dexterity, like completing jigsaws.

Because skills are neither secure nor automatic, a child around 5 to 11 years old with the disorder might have difficulty generalising them. Most typically developing learners find little difficulty in tasks such as adapting to catching various balls of different sizes. For individuals with DCD, adapting for such activities will be almost like learning a new skill each time. Tending to knock things over or bump into objects, they may be accident prone.

Older learners may be disorganised, finding it difficult to move around large buildings and to get to different parts of it punctually, especially if there are stairs to negotiate. In a school or college, some subjects pose challenges for example, safety implications where hazardous substances are handled. These will require risk assessments to be made for individual learners.

Commercial assessments

A variety of assessments is commercially available reflecting the varied nature and manifestations of DCD.

Used to identify visual motor problems associated with dyspraxia, the *Beery-Buktenica Developmental Test of Visual-Motor Integration – VMI* (Beery, Beery, and Buktenica, 2010) shows how well an individual can integrate visual and motor skills. It is standardised for ages 2 years to adult.

The *Movement Assessment Battery for Children* (second edition) or *Movement ABC-2* (Henderson, Sugden, and Barnett, 2007) contains eight tasks in each of three age ranges (3–6, 7–10, and 11–16 years). Covered are the three areas of manual dexterity, ball skills, and static and dynamic balance. Percentile scores are used to allow comparison of the child's scores with those of typically developing peers. A checklist covers ages 5 to 12 years and is a means of assessing movement in everyday situations.

An individually administered assessment of gross and fine motor skills, the *Bruinincks-Oseretsky Test of Motor Proficiency (BOT-2)* (Bruinincks and Bruinincks, 2005) is for ages 4 to 22 years. Eight subtests assess fine motor precision, fine motor integration, manual dexterity, bilateral co-ordination, balance, running speed and agility, upper limb co-ordination, and strength.

Standardised for the UK, the *Detailed Assessment of Speed of Handwriting – DASH* (Barnett, Henderson, Scheib, and Schulz, 2007) analyses the speed and legibility of handwriting. Used with ages 9 to 17 years, it identifies words per minute in relation to national averages, under both test and non-test conditions, giving a more accurate description of why the individual struggles to write legibly and at a normal speed. Occupational therapists use DASH to assess improvements made during therapy.

Subtests examine fine motor and precision skills, the speed of producing well-known symbolic material, the ability to alter speed of performance on two tasks with identical content, and free writing competency. DASH17+ is used for students aged 17 to 25 years in further and higher education.

Multi-professional assessments

Multi-professional assessments, like the range of commercial tests, reflect the complex nature of DCD. They may involve a physician, physical therapist/physiotherapist, occupational therapist, school psychologist, speech therapist/pathologist, and teacher. Such assessments recognise that movement and movement difficulties occur in a context.

Indeed, it is evident that 'movement is a product of innate (neurological), biological, and environmental factors (stimuli)' (Cairney, 2015). The individual is embedded in the task or the setting in which movement is being assessed (Ibid., p. 12, paraphrased). Accordingly, where possible several assessments are taken over time. This enables the assessor to consider variability in rates of change for the individual being assessed and those changes when compared with others of the same age (Ibid., p. 14).

Eligibility for special provision

In the United States, while DCD is not considered a designated learning disability, students may receive services within the education system based its impact on academic performance. In Canada, some parents have been able to acquire special education identification for their child under the umbrella of learning disability because of academic impact; or under the physical disability remit if the child raised self-care or safety concerns at school (Private communication, C. Missiuna, McMaster University, Ontario, 2010).

Curriculum and assessment

In institutions such as schools, colleges, and tuition centres, the curriculum for students with DCD is likely to be similar to that of most learners. There will be some differences of emphasis and of detail. Overall, the balance of subjects in the curriculum may emphasise areas where learners need extra practice and support.

Refinements may be made in programmes where motor co-ordination is central, including handwriting, physical education, art, geometry, and social and personal skills development. Craft or technology where tools are used, and laboratory work in science also require careful planning. This reflects the need for planning to be more detailed where the tasks are difficult for learners with DCD and helps ensure that activities where there is a risk of accident are made as safe as possible.

In developing planning, the educator will review learning sessions to highlight the motor skills that they require or that they develop. Teachers can then ensure that all learners can carry out the required motor activities, and that they are taught these directly where the skills are new. Taught individually or in small groups, these skills may be developed and practised during extra-curricular time in activity groups or clubs. Importantly, the skills should be developed and practised in context and regular opportunities provided to apply the skills in varied situations with different demands.

Assessment of motor development may be particularly detailed to ensure progress is monitored. Small steps of assessment will also help to demonstrate that some progress has been made so this can be recognised and affirmed.

Pedagogy

In this section, I look at

- general classroom approaches,
- specific skills training,
- accommodations to increase learner participation,
- physical education,
- personal and social education, and
- handwriting.

Clearly, the first three sections examine approaches, while the remaining three look at areas of learning that can be particularly challenging for those with DCD. In each of these areas, I describe combinations of motor skill teaching and accommodations to help participation and achievement. Specialised approaches used with learners having severe, complex difficulties associated with DCD and mainly delivered by occupational/physical therapists are discussed in a later section of this chapter, on therapy.

General group approaches

Missiuna, Polatajko, and Pollock (2015, pp. 218–232) suggest a framework for learning which includes a general approach to encouraging and teaching motor skills. It implies that educators and aides need to be trained to understand typical motor development in learners, the motor skills expected at different ages, and how these skills can be encouraged (Ibid., p. 220).

Accordingly, motor skills are promoted for all learners through general, curriculum-based activities. In planning a session where motor tasks will arise, the educator ensures that the necessary skills are directly taught in context. In a school or tuition centre, for example, this could involve cutting out shapes with scissors during an art or mathematics session. In helping ensure that everyone can participate in ball games, the skills of throwing and catching a ball would be directly taught (Missiuna, Polatajko, and Pollock, 2015, p. 220).

Implied in all this is a sort of universal design for learning applied to motor skills and development (Missiuna, Polatajko, and Pollock, 2015,

p. 220). A group room (such as a classroom in a school) is designed to promote motor development for example through changes in the physical environment. These might be exploration areas set up temporarily or for longer periods. To enable learners with DCD to reach the same learning goals as peers, a range of educational materials and approaches is used.

Consider that the learning goal is to improve fitness and participation in a physical activity. In this instance, the educator may need to find activities in which a learner with DCD can participate. The teacher might give the student a specific role that they can manage and later offer more demanding roles. Such approaches, while appropriate for all learners, are likely to especially benefit those with DCD. These roles should be part of the group activity which can sometimes require ingenuity. They should not be an isolated task where the student with DCD sits on the side lines deprived of the opportunity to develop team and social skills.

Specific skill training

General group approaches and specific teaching will not be sufficient to encourage the development of motor skills for all. A more focused group training in specific skills may be required. Missiuna, Polatajko, and Pollock (2015, p. 225) summarise some of the key aspects of what works in this respect.

They maintain that motor skills interventions are more effective

- when applied to learners over 5 years old,
- when specific skills training is a particular focus, and
- when the intervention is delivered in a group setting or through a home programme.

To have a positive impact, the intervention needs to be provided at least three times per week. In a school or tuition centre, the activities may take place during physical education sessions or as extra-curricular activities and can target learners having motor learning difficulties. Tsai, Wang, and Tseng (2009) report that they trained groups of children in the motor skills required in the game of football. Subsequently, they found that the task performance of children with DCD improved.

Accommodations to increase participation

Accommodations (as distinguished from 'modifications') are physical or environmental changes such as giving more time to complete a task, allowing short breaks within the time set for the task, changing the layout of the room or area, and using computer software to 'read' text to the learner. These enable the learner to work round a potential difficulty.

Accommodations may be used to enable a learner with DCD to participate in activities and to make progress in acquiring motor skills. These may be developed as the teacher, occupational therapist, and physical therapist work together.

Resources may be adjusted, or different resources may be used. Saving a student the labour of typing every word in a report or essay, predictive computer software can be used. At a low-tech level, a pencil grip can help the learner control the fine motor movements of handwriting. Paper with guidance lines can enable the learner to keep their writing within acceptable parameters. In physical education, a larger ball might be used to make catching manageable and perhaps over time reduced in size as the learner develops the skills of catching.

Detailed steps of an activity might be taught while retaining its overall purpose and context. In cooking, the exact steps of making pastry may be taught. This may be done using behavioural chaining, an instructional procedure used to reinforce (increase the likelihood of) individual responses that occur in a sequence. Each step is prompted by verbal, visual, and physical prompts. As the learner makes progress, these prompts are gradually withdrawn.

Environmental changes such as ensuring the teaching area is not cluttered and that there is space to move across the room can help the learner with DCD. Such changes are discussed later in this chapter in the section 'Organisation'.

Physical education

The importance of physical health and physical activity

While physical activity and physical health are important, individuals with DCD struggle with organised sport and free play. This is owing to gross motor difficulties relating to balance, poor eye-hand co-ordination, and poor skills in catching and throwing and kicking.

Accordingly, learners with DCD tend to avoid such activities, so limiting opportunities for physical and social development. Leading to poorer opportunities for friendship and socialisation, lost play can ultimately create isolation. As well, lack of play and participation in sports and physical activities diminish physical health (Cairney, 2015, pp. 62–63).

DCD and challenges of physical education and activity

Evident for all is the importance of physical education, physical activity, and the enjoyment of sports and play. For those with DCD there are challenges. Skipping with or without a rope may be difficult. Riding a bicycle involving balance, co-ordination, and constantly processing and responding to visual information for steering is hard for someone with DCD and tends to take longer to accomplish. Posing difficulties moving about among apparatus, physical education sessions may be unwelcome. Problems judging distance and velocity make many ball games daunting.

Strategies in physical education sessions

In physical education sessions, such as gymnastics, the teacher can ensure that there is a space for each learner to which they may return. Providing a reassuring sense of predictability and security, this can help to build confidence. Floor markings can be used to indicate the paths that students are expected to follow to help with orientation and direction.

Changing into appropriate clothing for physical education and changing back into day clothes afterwards can be laborious. Time limits where this is expected to be done quickly can add to the pressure involved. To help with this, learners can use adapted clothing using false buttons and Velcro fasteners. With such items the adaptations can be discrete, and the clothing can still be smart and fashionable.

Adapted Physical Education

Adapted Physical Education is 'an individualised programme including physical and motor fitness, fundamental motor skills and patterns, skills in aquatics and dance, and individual and group games and sports designed to meet the unique needs of individuals' (Winnick, 2010, p. 4).

An Adapted Physical Education teacher concentrates on fundamental motor skills and physical performance of individual learners. This may involve working with learners for a certain number of designated hours per week. In a school for example, a classroom teacher and the Adapted Physical Education teacher can work together to develop and teach programmes of physical education as well as leisure and recreation.

Benefiting students with DCD, such approaches also help others, for example, those with health or orthopaedic impairments (www.teachinga daptedpe.com).

Personal and social development

DCD and potential limitations on leisure activities and socialising

Co-ordination difficulties hamper involvement in team games requiring high levels of motor co-ordination, some computer games, and board games. Poor co-ordination may inhibit participation in social activities such as dancing, ice-skating, and bowling, limiting opportunities to socialise and participate. Teachers and others should be able to identify at least one sport or activity that the learner is motivated to try. This can then become the focus, while teaching the motor skills involved directly and in context.

Handling money

In using money visiting a cinema, a dance venue, or when shopping, older individuals may use debit or credit cards which, depending on the amount, may allow contactless payments. For younger children, or where physical cash is required, handling small coins can be problematic particularly if one is under time pressure at the front of a busy line. Taught directly, such activity can then be practised in various settings.

Domestic skills

Domestic skills, such as cleaning a room, keeping an area tidy, cooking, laying a table, and arranging shelf contents, pose challenges relating to co-ordination and movement. Often adaptations in routines or in the use of items of equipment can help. In preparing a meal, using a hand can-opener may be tricky but a wall can-opener should be much easier to operate. Applying butter or other spread on bread or biscuits can be difficult but using cutlery with thick rubber handles is a possible adaptation.

Personal hygiene and personal appearance

Both personal hygiene and personal appearance can influence peer acceptance and self-esteem. Individuals with DCD may have difficulty with washing hair, cleaning teeth, and cutting fingernails. For younger students, using the toilet may be problematic.

Dressing and undressing can take an inordinate amount of time for individuals with DCD. False buttons above Velcro fasteners on clothing, and trousers with an elasticised waist, can save time. If a learner needs to use the toilet in education settings where recreational times are limited, such adaptations can be helpful.

In high school, hygiene may still be hard to achieve consistently. Girls may find changing sanitary products difficult. Requiring sensitive guidance from parents and the school, they may find it hard to apply facial cosmetics sparingly so that the effect is inadvertently smeared and garish. Some of these skills can be taught in school and at home. Intimate aspects of hygiene may be more appropriately taught by parents with advice from a physical or occupational therapist.

Encouraging self-worth

Learners with DCD can become frustrated and demoralised and come to have low self-worth partly because of the persistent difficulties they face that may not always be understood by others. In these circumstances teachers and others will try to establish the root cause of the behaviour. They will try to understand DCD and enhance their own skills in supporting students, improving the likelihood that the learner will be able to meet the challenges of education and other day-to-day demands.

Handwriting and alternatives

Dysgraphia

'Dysgraphia' refers to learning disorder related to difficulties with handwriting 'such as forming letters or words or writing within a defined space' (Pullen, Lane, Ashworth, and Lovelace, 2011, p. 191). In teaching handwriting, the principles already discussed apply, namely, teaching explicitly and directly, rather than expecting the learner to acquire the skill by watching others. Writing is taught in context and for a purpose. In the physical aspects of handwriting, support may be provided by a physiotherapist/physical therapist or an occupational therapist.

Writing posture and positioning

To avoid discomfort and improve performance, a learner with DCD may need to be taught a good writing posture. Desks and chairs should be the correct size in the sense that both the writer's feet can rest flat on the floor and the desk height is slightly above the elbows. Positioning the paper to be written on should align it with the writer's arm. To help ensure that the position is maintained marks can be put on the desk or a large card template may be used (Mather, Wendling, and Roberts, 2009, pp. 89–90).

Writing implements

Helping the writer to hold the utensil more comfortably, a three-cornered pencil grip or a pen with a rubber finger grip can be used. Pencil pressure on the paper may be too light or too heavy because of proprioceptive difficulties affecting co-ordination and the sense of exerting pressure. A pen that illuminates when pressed for writing can help the writer become more aware of the pressure exerted. An individual pressing too lightly will be encouraged to increase pressure to make the implement light up. By contrast, a writer pressing too heavily will be expected to reduce it so as not to illuminate the pen.

Lined paper

Students can work on pre-writing patterns to help develop the rhythm and fluency necessary for writing. When learning to write letters of the alphabet, using a special lined paper can help the formation of the correct shapes. This specially printed paper has a central line and a line above and below. The upper line indicates the height of the ascending letter and the lower line signifies the depth of the descending letter. Mather, Wendling and Roberts (2009, pp. 91–93) provide further suggestions to help develop good letter formation.

Movement control

With regard to movement control, learners must know the forms of letters and how they join cursively. Because of processing difficulties, they may have difficulty stopping a letter. They may run the line of a letter on so that, for example, a 'c' has a bottom tail that is far too long. It follows from this that the writer must learn that the letters have a beginning and an end. This can be helped by providing some practice writing a series of letters in a specified short horizontal line in which the start and finish are marked by vertical lines. Such drill-like activities can be made more engaging if the teacher makes clear the purpose of the task and its importance. Also, the activity can be kept short and repeated at intervals rather than being a long and laboured task.

Where letters and words are poorly spaced, cursive writing can be introduced early and the writer can be encouraged to leave a finger space between words. This works best when using a pencil rather than a pen (which may smudge). Fluency in writing is difficult to attain for a learner with DCD.

Moving from pre-writing patterns to the formation of letters with joins/integral exit strokes to cursive writing can assist fluency. The learner is not taught to write 'separate' letters. Teachers may also consider using commercial writing programmes.

Alternatives to handwriting

Given the difficulties of handwriting for individuals with DCD, some may think that the effort necessary to accomplish good handwriting is hardly worth it. This may be reinforced by knowing that computer-aided alternatives are available. Even business contracts can now be 'signed' electronically. However, the skill of handwriting has not been replaced by computer alternatives and remains necessary in many situations. Furthermore, alternatives are not problem free.

Several computer-based strategies are available for bypassing handwriting problems, but each has its own demands which learners may find challenging. Examples include

- using a keyboard,
- dictation with a voice recognition system, and
- word prediction programmes.

Keyboard skills are an alternative to handwriting. But a learner must be able to automatically use the letter finding skills and keyboard skills involved in word processing. Otherwise, word processing may not be fluent enough to be a viable alternative.

Dictation using a voice recognition system can eventually lead to better and longer text than a learner may produce by handwriting. Nevertheless, it still involves learners mastering the commands for monitoring and correcting errors. They must be able to dictate, monitor if there have been any errors, and use the programme commands effectively. All this places considerable demands on working memory.

In word prediction software the 'predictions' are based around syntax, spelling, and the frequent or recent use of words. However, the software may also pose difficulties for individuals having poor working memory or problems with attention or executive function. This is because the learner must monitor the list of options that changes with each letter that is typed.

Resources

Aids to more fluent writing include pencil grips and illuminating pens as described earlier in this chapter. Special equipment for physical education may be used such as extra light balls and extra-large bats. Adapted equipment like cutlery with thick rubber handles may be employed. False buttons above Velcro fasteners may be attached to clothing, and trousers may have an elasticised waist.

As well as sometimes using special resources, students' participation and achievement can be enhanced by using existing resources differently. An example is decreasing the distance between the thrower and catcher when passing a ball so that the task is easier, then extending the distance as the necessary skills and confidence are developed.

Therapy

Involving team working and examples of specialist interventions, approaches to therapy can be identified as follows:

- innovative multi-professional working;
- Neuromotor Task Training; and
- Cognitive Orientation to Daily Occupational Performance.

Innovative multi-professional working

Good opportunities for innovative team working arise between the teacher of physical education and a physical therapist or occupational therapist. Since DCD affects activities of daily living, the occupational therapist has an important role. Working individually with the student for some of the time, therapists will also work with the teacher, parents, and others so that all concerned can ensure that motor skills are encouraged and applied in different contexts.

In current practice there is a tendency to move away from 'bottom-up' approaches, such as perceptual motor training, which attempt to remediate supposed underlying motor deficits, expecting this to lead to improvements in motor performance. Evidence of effectiveness of such bottom-up strategies tends to be weak. Accordingly, and increasingly, 'top-down' approaches are preferred which focus a goal and on the context of the motor learning. Being able to tie a shoelace or being able to pass a ball accurately in a basketball game are examples having a goal and a context.

Neuromotor Task Training

Neuromotor Task Training was developed in the Netherlands for the treatment of children with DCD by paediatric physical therapists

(Niemeijer, Smits-Engelsman, and Schoemaker, 2007). Based on motor control and motor learning principles, it also takes account of principles of motor teaching and motivation. Fundamental to the approach is a neuro-motor assessment and a task analysis of the skills that the individual child finds problematic.

As a task specific intervention, Neuromotor Task Training focuses directly on teaching the skills that the individual needs in daily life. Tasks are learned in a variety of contexts to help the child generalise the skills involved to real-life settings. Learning is directed by the physical or occupational therapist, who gives spoken instructions, visual prompts, or physical assistance, to help the learner to get the feeling of the movement and to learn it.

Cognitive Orientation to Daily Occupational Performance

Developed in Canada for children with DCD, Cognitive Orientation to Daily Occupational Performance (CO-OP) (Levac, Wishart, Missiuna, and Wright, 2009) typically involves an occupational therapist working closely with parents and the student. It aims to help children discover the cognitive strategies that will improve their ability to carry out everyday tasks such as handwriting, riding a bicycle, using cutlery, and catching a ball.

CO-OP employs global and domain specific strategies and guides individuals to discover strategies, enabling them to achieve the goals they have selected. Used to determine when a student has difficulties per-forming an activity, 'dynamic performance analysis' makes it possible to identify points where performance breaks down. The therapist teaches the student a global strategy called 'Goal-Plan-Do-Check' to act as a framework for solving motor-based performance problems, then guides the student to discover domain specific strategies that will enable the activity to be performed.

Organisation

Group organisation can be a vehicle to encourage younger children to develop and practice motor skills. In a larger group setting such as a school classroom, there may be several activity centres where children can be shown and taught fine motor and gross motor skills. In play areas, teachers can directly teach children the skills needed to participate.

Also, the physical organisation of larger group settings can help miti-gate the effects of DCD. It can ensure relatively free movement around the room without unnecessary clutter. The student may sit close to the front of the group in a seat near to the entry door to avoid bumping into others and into objects when they enter or leave the room. Ideally, the room will be large enough to allow furniture arrangements for different activities such as group work or whole class work to be laid out permanently.

This enables the learner with DCD to become accustomed to the layout rather than having to constantly adapt as furniture is moved into different arrangements for new activities. However, if space is limited, stable layouts may not be possible. In this situation, the positions into which furniture is moved for different activities can be marked on the floor of the room so that the positions are at least predictable and consistent.

Conclusion

Understanding DCD, dyspraxia, and types of motor difficulties began with notions of clumsiness, as reflected in their definitions. Dyspraxia tends to be defined in terms of the planning and organisation of movement. DCD has a pervasive detrimental effect on many aspects of daily life. In children aged 5 to 11 years, the prevalence of DCD is 5% to 6%. It may be more common in boys. DCD co-occurs with many other conditions sometimes very strongly as with attention deficit hyperactivity disorder.

DCD may have a genetic element. It may originate prenatally or soon after birth and may result from damage as the brain is developing. Preterm birth appears to be a risk factor. DCD may be associated with dysfunction of the parietal lobes and the cerebellum. In children, neurological mechanisms involved in predicting motor control may be compromised and there may be deficits in executive control.

Identification and assessment can involve the use of screening instruments, standardised tests, and multi-professional assessments. There are implications for tests at different ages, and eligibility for special provision.

Curricula for learners with DCD tend to differ in emphasis and in detail from that of other learners. It may emphasise areas where learners need extra practice and support. Programmes may specify achievement in greater detail where motor co-ordination is central, and where tasks are difficult or potentially unsafe for learners with DCD. Required motor activities are taught directly and in context where necessary. Detailed assessment of motor development is carried out, allowing progress to be monitored, recognised, and affirmed.

Pedagogy involves general classroom approaches, specific skills training, and accommodations to increase student participation. It also relates to key areas including physical education, personal and social education, and handwriting.

Resources include special and adapted equipment as well as the use of regular resources in a different way. Examples of physical therapy are Neuromotor Task Training and Cognitive Orientation to Daily Occupational Performance. Suitable organisation includes the layout of furniture and equipment in rooms.

Thinking points

Readers may wish to consider

- the effectiveness of approaches that will help students with DCD across all areas of school life and, in particular, subject lessons, and
- how teachers, classroom aides, and others can work more effectively with physical therapists and occupational therapists to enhance overall provision.

Key text

Cairney, J. (2015) (Ed.) *Developmental Coordination Disorder and Its Consequences*.
    Toronto, Canada, University of Toronto Press.
    Intended for teachers, parents, and physicians, this book includes information on diagnosis, the consequences concerning mental health, social functioning, and physical health and activity, and the neuropsychological foundations of DCD. As the title suggests, there is an emphasis on the consequences of DCD.

References

American Psychiatric Association (2013) *Diagnostic and Statistical Manual of Mental Disorders Fifth Edition (DSM-5)*. Washington DC, APA.

Barnett, A., Henderson, S. E., Scheib, B., and Schulz, J. (2007) *The Detailed Assessment of Speed of Handwriting – DASH*. Pearson Clinical.

Beery, K. E., Beery, N. A., and Buktenica, N. A. (2010) *The Beery-Buktenica Developmental Test of Visual-Motor Co-ordination*. Pearson Clinical.

Bruinincks, R. H. and Bruinincks, B. D. (2005) *Bruinincks-Oseretsky Test of Motor Proficiency (BOT-2)*. Easel, TX, AGS Publishing.

Cairney, J. (2015) 'Developmental coordination disorder, physical activity, and physical health: Results from the PHAST project' in Cairney, J. (Ed.) *Developmental Coordination Disorder and Its Consequences*. Toronto, CA, University of Toronto Press.

Edwards, J., Berube, M., Erlandson, K., Haug, S.*et al.* (2011) 'Developmental coordination disorder in school-aged children born very preterm and/or at very low birth weight: A systematic review'. *Journal of Developmental and Behavioural Pediatrics* 32, 9, 678–687 (November).

Engel-Yeger, B. (2015) 'DCD and participation' in Cairney, J. (Ed.) *Developmental Coordination Disorder and Its Consequences.* Toronto, CA, University of Toronto Press.

Gaines, R., Collins, D., Boycott, K.*et al.* (2008) 'Clinical expression of developmental coordination disorder in a large Canadian family'. *Paediatrics and Health* 13, 9, 763–768 (November).

Geuze, R. H. (2005) 'Postural control in children with developmental coordination disorder'. *Neural Plasticity* 12, 2–3, 183–196, discussion 263–272.

Henderson, S. E., Sugden, D. A., and Barnett, A. L. (2007) *Movement Assessment Battery for Children (MABC-2).* London, Pearson.

Levac, D., Wishart, L., Missiuna, C., and Wright, V. (2009) 'The application of motor learning strategies within functionally based interventions for children with neuromotor conditions'. *Pediatric Physical Therapy* 21, 4, 345–355 (Winter).

Mather, N. and Wending, B. J. (2012) *Essentials of dyslexia assessment and intervention.* Hoboken, NJ, Wiley.

Mather, N., Wending, B. J. and Roberts, R. (2009) *Writing Assessment and Instruction for Students with Learning Disabilities.* San Francisco, Jossey-Bass.

Missiuna, C., Polatajko, H. J., and Pollock, N. (2015) 'Strategic management of children with developmental coordination disorder' in Cairney, J. (Ed.) *Developmental Coordination Disorder and Its Consequences.* Toronto, CA, University of Toronto Press.

Niemeijer, A. S., Smits-Engelsman, B. C., and Schoemaker, M. M. (2007) 'Neuromotor task training for children with developmental coordination disorder: A controlled trial'. *Developmental Medicine and Child Neurology* 49, 6, 406–411 (June).

Piek, J. P. and Rigoli, D. (2015) 'Psychosocial and behavioural difficulties' in Cairney, J. (Ed.) *Developmental Coordination Disorder and Its Consequences.* Toronto, CA, University of Toronto Press.

Pullen, P. C., Lane, H. B., Ashworth, K. E., and Lovelace, S. P. (2011) 'Learning disabilities' in Kauffman, J. M. and Hallahan, D. P. (Eds.) *Handbook of Special Education.* New York and London, Routledge.

Schoemaker, M. M. and Wilson, B. N. (2015) 'Screening for developmental coordination disorder in school-age children' in Cairney, J. (Ed.) *Developmental Coordination Disorder and Its Consequences.* Toronto, CA, University of Toronto Press.

Tsai, C. L., Wang, C. H. and Tseng, Y-T. (2012) 'Effects of exercise intervention on event-related potential and task performance indices of attention networks in children with developmental coordination disorder'. Brain and Cognition79, 1, 12–22.

Wilson, P. (2005) 'Visuospatial, kinesthetic, visuomotor integration, and visuoconstructional disorders: Implications for motor development' in Dewey, D. and Tupper, D. E. (Eds.) *Developmental Disorders: A Neurological Perspective.* New York, The Guilford Press.

Wilson, P. H. (2015) 'Neurocognitive processing deficits' in Cairney, J. (Ed.) *Developmental Coordination Disorder and Its Consequences*. Toronto, CA, University of Toronto Press.

Winnick, J. P. (2010) *Adapted Physical Education and Sport*. 5th edition. Chapaign, IL, Human Kinetics Publishers.

Zwicker, J. G., Missiuna, C., Harris, S. R., and Boyd, L. A. (2010a) 'Brain activation associated with motor skills practice in children with developmental coordination disorder: An fMRI study'. *International Journal of Developmental Neuroscience* 29, 2, 145–152 (April).

Zwicker, J. G., Missiuna, C., Harris, S. R., and Boyd, L. A. (2010b) 'Brain activation of children with developmental coordination disorder is different than peers'. *Pediatrics* 126, 3, e678-e686 (September).

Chapter 6

Multi-professional working

Introduction

Policies in children and family services have long called for a more 'joined-up outcomes-based approach' to delivering services. This is expected to be founded on precise processes of 'referral, recording, information sharing, assessment, management, planning, delivery, monitoring and evaluation' (Davis and Smith, 2012, Chapter 1).

In this chapter, as a preamble to examining multi-professional working, I examine the roles of the various professionals potentially working with special learners. Looking at examples relevant to provision for individuals with specific learning disorders, I consider speech pathologists, physical therapists/physiotherapists, school/educational psychologists, occupational therapists, and school social workers.

Discussed are multi-professional collaboration including multi-agency working, different service delivery models, and common links across services. I examine the challenges of multi-professional working, especially co-ordinating numerous professionals, and dealing with professional differences.

Aids to good multi-professional working are considered. These are developing overlapping perspectives, sharing a joint purpose, as well as communicating clearly, having agreed responsibilities, developing a one stop venue for parents and students, forming strong parent–professional relationships, participating in shared training and assessments, working together in the school classroom, and co-ordinating support. This chapter draws on the fuller discussion of multi-professional working in *Looking into Special Education* (Farrell, 2014, pp. 89–108).

Professional roles

Many professional roles and responsibilities are involved in working with special students. They include administrator, advocate, art therapist,

DOI: 10.4324/9781003177975-6

audiologist, behaviour therapist, child and adolescent psychiatrist, classroom aide, clinical psychologist, cognitive-behavioural therapist, conductor (involved in conductive education), counsellor, dance and movement therapist, school psychologist, music therapist, neurologist, ophthalmologist, orthoptist, paediatrician, prosthetists, school social worker, and teacher (Farrell, 2009, passim).

Various professionals contribute to provision for specific learning disorders each with its own insights, training, and remit. Examples are

- speech pathologist,
- physical therapist,
- school psychologist,
- occupational therapist, and
- school social worker.

Speech-language pathologist

'Speech-language pathologist' is the term used in the US while 'speech and language therapist' is preferred in England and 'speech pathologist' in Australia. Their work involves assessing and treating disorders affecting an individual's speech, language, voice, swallowing, and mental processing to improve communication. Interventions may include practice and exercises and providing support with communication aids such as manual signing or using symbols.

A speech-language pathologist may qualify through a degree or diploma course. In the US, different states regulate practice under state laws. The basic standard required by the American Speech Language Hearing Association (2021) for certified speech-language pathology membership is a degree in speech-language pathology, a clinical fellowship year, and passing a further examination.

A qualified speech-language pathologist may work in a school, clinic, or hospital. In a school, they often work closely in a team with teachers and others. They may work directly with a student or in a consultancy role with a teacher and parents who contribute to interventions to improve the learner's communication.

Physical therapist

A physical therapist in the US (physiotherapist in England) is a health professional who has undergone training and has received certification. They may be based in a hospital or community clinic and may visit schools or clients' homes and provide treatment to improve posture and movement and particular functions relating to them. This may be done through exercises, movement, positioning, physical aids, hydrotherapy, and the use of vibration or warmth. Specialisms include developmental physical therapy with special children, and rehabilitative physical therapy.

A developmental physical therapist will carry out an assessment of a child's level of functioning and physical abilities and develop a treatment plan that often involves contributions from other adults. Those caring for the child will take note of the physical therapist's advice on positioning, exercises, and the use of appliances and aids. Paediatric physical therapy involves the treatment of children with conditions such as cerebral palsy, spina bifida, and juvenile arthritis.

Professional bodies include the American Physical Therapy Association (2021) and in the UK the Chartered Society of Physiotherapy (2021).

School psychologist

School psychology is essentially psychology applied to children's learning and development in the context of their schooling. A school psychologist (in England an 'educational psychologist') applies the skills and knowledge of educational and clinical psychology. They carry out assessment and interventions to help children and young people develop and learn better. Postgraduate training is likely to include the study of assessments and their interpretation, child development, personality, child and adolescent learning, the social psychology of groups, and the wider organisation of schooling.

Working closely with teachers and others, a school psychologist may observe students in classroom settings and advise teachers on suitable approaches to learning and behaviour management. Among professional associations are the Association of Educational Psychologists in the UK (2021) and in the US the National Association of School Psychologists (2021).

Occupational therapist

An occupational therapist treats perceptual, motor, and motor learning disorders. Occupational therapy concerns assessing and intervening in response to various requirements arising from physical disabilities, psychological difficulties, and problems with sensory awareness, perceptual skills, and motor awareness.

An occupational therapist can provide therapy, aids, and adaptations which may involve implementing training programmes for self-help, work, and leisure skills. Paediatric occupational therapists work with families and schools to maximise students' abilities at home and at school. Professional bodies include O T Australia (2021) and the American Occupational Therapy Association (2021).

School social worker

School social workers address social and psychological issues hindering a learner's academic progress. In the US, training and qualification may be through specialist degree courses followed by licensing. Through counselling, crisis intervention and prevention programmes, school social workers help young people overcome life difficulties, improving their chances of succeeding in school.

They help young people with academic problems and assist others whose social, psychological, emotional, or physical difficulties put them at risk, such as students with physical or mental health disabilities. A school social worker may be involved in violence-prevention programmes. They also have a working knowledge of relevant law, and advocacy skills. The largest social work professional body is the National Association of Social Workers (2021) based in Washington DC.

Multi-professional working

Multi-professional and multi-agency working

Multi-professional working and a subset of it, multi-agency working can be distinguished. In multi-professional working, professionals holding different perspectives and backgrounds work together successfully as a team or organisation. Sharing a common enterprise of day-to-day practice, assessment, or liaison they work for to benefit individuals with disabilities and disorders. Such working may involve professionals from the same agency as when in an education service a teacher and classroom aide work together, or when a nurse, physician, and physiotherapist cooperate within a health service. Extra challenges are posed by multi-agency working where professionals from different services work together for example health, social services/welfare, youth justice services, and education.

Service delivery models

Multi-agency working can range from periodic meetings to highly integrated working in a single venue. A multi-agency panel might meet monthly. Members of different services might be seconded to a multi-agency team, full- or part-time, perhaps to a team concerned with challenging student behaviour.

Integrated services might work in a single location, developing a common approach involving extended schools, full-service schools or children's centres. Special schools can be useful hubs for this, offering opportunities for better communication because of the common venue and opportunities to train together and develop a more holistic approach to the individual.

Common links across services

Some links across and between services are comparatively common. School (educational) psychologists tend to work with staff from social/welfare services like school and community social workers and staff from community health services. Staff members responsible for school attendance liaise with social workers who know the respective families. Specialist hospital physicians work with teachers for students with sensory impairments. Teachers educating learners having language impairments form partnerships with speech pathologists/therapists, while educators of students with physical disabilities cooperate with occupational therapists. Education-based staff working with students having conduct disorders or anxiety or depressive disorders liaise with mental health professionals.

In different countries the exact arrangements and inter relationships vary but essentially a typical range of professional relationships are likely to be formed.

Other less common relationships that have the potential to be beneficial to a special student may require extra effort and planning. Networks of charities and national or local/state initiatives may encourage better professional partnerships.

Challenges of multi-professional working

Among advantages of good multi-professional working are meeting the requirements of children and their families, and ensuring improved outcomes for them, as well as benefits for staff and services. While there are many areas of good practice, attempts to secure multi-disciplinary and multi-agency working too often fall short.

Challenges of co-ordinating numerous professionals

Part of the challenge is dealing with the sheer number of professionals drawn in. Just to take one example, for someone experiencing traumatic brain injury, a large team of professionals is initially involved. This may include medical personnel (physician, nurse), nutritionist or dietician, psychologist, speech and language pathologist/therapist, teacher, occupational therapist, recreational therapist, physical therapist/physiotherapist, a social worker, and a swallowing therapist (a speech pathologist who undertakes swallowing assessments and provides advice on safe feeding). As the child makes progress, the team becomes smaller, perhaps being reduced to a physician, teacher, psychologist, and social worker.

Professional differences from salaries to power struggles

Among inhibitors of good multi-professional working is different professionals' training, perspectives, aims, and responsibilities. Health and social care may have different local organisation arrangements and different links to national government. Geographical boundaries covered by various services may not coincide creating potential problems where there is overlap or gaps in service coverage. Power struggles and self-indulgent personality clashes can sour joint working. Management structures, educational background, perspectives, priorities, and salaries differ. Notions of confidentiality, where information ought to be shared, can be over-precious.

Aids to multi-professional working

Features that enhance multi-professional working include

- developing overlapping perspectives,
- sharing a joint purpose and communicating clearly,
- having agreed responsibilities,
- developing a one stop venue for parents and students,
- forming strong parent–professional relationships,
- participating in shared training and assessments,
- working together in the school classroom, and
- co-ordinating support.

Developing overlapping perspectives

While congruent perspectives between members of different professions may be unachievable, overlapping viewpoints can be developed. Consider multi-professional working between teachers and a speech-language pathologist/speech therapist with a student having speech and communication disorders. Here the speech-language pathologist's perspective (for example, a psycholinguistic view of communication) will be informed by specific training and expertise. Any such perspectives will influence the frameworks for understanding for speech and language development, pathology, and remediation which will in turn influence clinical terminology ('dysarthria', 'verbal dyspraxia', 'dysphonia', and 'dysphasia').

The educational overview of teachers and others may differ from that of the speech therapist. Where this is so, teacher and speech pathologist, school psychologist, and others must work closely together to ensure that their aims coincide and that the educational and speech pathology terminology and perspectives are integrated for proposed interventions.

Sharing a joint purpose and communicating clearly

Where the purpose of multi-professional working is unclear, it is less likely to be fulfilled because no one will know when the goal is near. Clear practical needs should influence the size and make-up of a team of professionals co-ordinating and delivering provision. In a well-organised Individualised Education Programme meeting, the purpose and the respective roles of the learner, parent, and professionals will be clearly understood. After the meeting, there should be evaluation and monitoring to help determine the effectiveness or otherwise of the proposed actions.

Jargon creeps so invidiously into all professions that professionals may be unaware of the acronyms, special expressions, or unusual terms that they use and which muddy communication. As some unfortunate speaker once advised, 'avoid jargon like the plague!'.

Having agreed responsibilities

All professionals must be well-informed about the contribution of other colleagues and how they can work together to benefit of the individual learner and their family. Responsibilities of individual professionals can be specified and linked to the academic and personal progress that students make. A school seeking the services of an educational/school psychologist may be able to link their work to learner outcomes.

Consider a psychologist helping a school introduce a system of behaviour management expected to improve the behaviour of learners with oppositional defiance disorder. An agreed outcome might be a reduction in the number of learners excluded from school annually. Teachers' opinions could be gathered before and after the introduction of the intervention to see if their view of learner's behaviour improves. This helps to assess the efficacy of the intervention enabling school and psychologist focus on the task and their respective roles in achieving desired aims.

Developing a one stop venue for parents and learners

For special learners, many professionals may be involved, making it worth considering the use of a single 'one stop' centre. Here staff could draw together information and advice to inform educational and other judgements to help the student to learn and develop best.

This centre may be a special school, a mainstream school, a clinic or similar. Practical advantages for parents and students will be apparent. Instead of needing to separately visit a hospital, a clinic, and a therapist's office, all the relevant professionals can be seen in one venue. For their part, professionals can schedule time to talk, share information and work together as necessary. Potential drawbacks are that a particular professional may find it harder to keep in touch with colleagues in the same field (say psychology) and may lack the support, information, and shared vision of single professional groups at their best. This suggests that some of the time in a typical week could be spent with colleagues of the same profession where issues require it.

Forming strong parent–professional relationships

Parents may be unprepared for the many professionals they encounter when their child is assessed with a disability or disorder and be temporarily disorientated. They will value emotional support, practical help, and clear information at this time. Parents and professionals develop good partnerships when they value each other's involvement, and when professionals recognise that the parent may be highly knowledgeable about their child's specific disorder. Discussions should be realistic, involve practical advice and listening, and recognise a learner's strengths and weakness. Parents appreciate professionals who do not have pre-conceived ideas of what the child can do. Parents find talking to staff when dropping the child at school useful as well as the use of e-mails, phone calls, occasional meetings, and a daily log help home–school communication. Parents often help each other, sharing similar experiences and professionals may facilitate this.

Participating in shared training and assessments

Joint training may be offered to several different professional groups so long as it is well-planned, and it is clear what each group will gain from it. Speech and language therapists/pathologists, teachers, and aides working with students having speech and language disorders may attend joint conferences and training to hear about and discuss new approaches or research. Regional conferences can offer a useful source of information and sharing for professionals from surrounding areas.

Joint assessments of the learning and development of special students can involve various professionals. Rather than each professional assessing the student individually, contemporaneous assessments can be made. In such arrangements, the professionals communicate with the student and each other to try to better understand the student's learning and development and what can enhance these. As three or four separate assessments are replaced by one detailed and holistic assessment, this approach also saves time.

Working together in the school classroom

Joint working between teacher and classroom aid/teaching assistant is central. The aide may work predominantly with special learners. In a preparing role, they help the teacher plan work or get curriculum materials ready. Organisationally, they arrange the classroom to enable work to be pitched accurately for different learners and groups. Managerially, they help general behaviour management, keeping individual learners focused on their work. Practically, they work with individuals or groups, give extra explanations, and support the outcomes of Individual Education Plans.

When the teacher is speaking to the whole class, the aide might note the contributions of different learners to ensure equitable participation over time, feeding this information into subsequent teacher planning. Teachers' lesson planning should indicate the aide's role in assisting learners to reach the lesson outcomes and this (like the teacher's contribution) can be evaluated. In the US, a classroom teacher and an 'adapted physical education teacher' work together to develop and teach programmes of physical education as well as leisure and recreation, helping to include learners with DCD, or health or orthopaedic impairments.

Co-ordinating support

One person being responsible for co-ordinating support to a learner can help reduce service duplication and expose gaps in provision. In England, a special educational needs co-ordinator (SENCO) is a teacher bringing together support and interventions within and beyond school. For teachers, parents and learners within the school who have concerns about progress and provision they are the point of contact. Beyond school, SENCOs help to co-ordinate the support of professionals like psychologists, physicians, physiotherapists, occupational therapists, and mental health workers. Other countries appoint staff with similar roles.

Co-ordinators must know learners and their families. This enables them to evaluate changes to the learner's well-being or academic progress noticed by themselves or reported to them by others. Also, co-ordinators must know what local services can be deployed and have the professional credibility to bring together professionals with competing commitments.

Meetings called to frame or to review an Individual Education Program (IEP) can assist multi-professional collaboration especially if there is a clear agenda, explicit roles for each participant, and agreement about what the outcomes of the meeting should be.

Thinking points

With reference to services that you work in or that you know of, identify two or three challenges to effective multi-professional working. For each challenge, try to identify what could be done to improve matters. What time scale and resources would likely be involved?

Key texts

Davis, J. and Smith, M. (2012) *Working in Multi-professional Contexts: A Practical Guide for Professionals In Children's Services.* London, Sage.

Drawing on examples from the UK, this book covers key areas of multi-professional working.

Conclusion

Among professionals potentially working with special students some often work with individuals with specific learning disorders. These are the speech pathologist, physical therapist/physiotherapist, school/educational psychologist, occupational therapist, and school social worker. Multi-professional collaboration includes multi-agency working, different service delivery models, and common links across services.

Challenges include co-ordinating numerous professionals and dealing with friction ranging from salary differences to power struggles. Aids to good multi-professional working are developing overlapping perspectives, sharing a joint purpose, and communicating clearly, having agreed responsibilities, developing a one stop venue for parents and students, forming strong parent–professional relationships, participating in shared training and assessments, working together in the school classroom, and co-ordinating support.

References

American Occupational Therapy Association (2021) www.aota.org.

American Physical Therapy Association (2021) www.apta.org.

American Speech Language Hearing Association (2021) www.asha.org.

Association of Educational Psychologists (2021) www.aep.org.uk.

Chartered Society of Physiotherapy (2021) www.csp.org.uk.

Davis, J. and Smith, M. (2012) *Working in Multi-professional Contexts: A Practical Guide for Professionals In Children's Services*. London, Sage.

Farrell, M. (2009) *Foundations of Special Education: An Introduction*. London, Wiley-Blackwell.

Farrell, M. (2014) *Looking into Special Education: A Synthesis of Key Themes and Concepts*. New York and London, Routledge.

National Association of School Psychologists (2021) www.naspweb.org.

National Association of Social Workers (2021) www.naswdc.org.

O T Australia (2021) www.auscot.com.au.

Index

For Product Safety Concerns and Information please contact our EU
representative GPSR@taylorandfrancis.com
Taylor & Francis Verlag GmbH, Kaufingerstraße 24, 80331 München, Germany